Family Bicycling in the Washington-Baltimore Area

To Carole, Kevin and Lauren, my cycling partners forever

Family Bicycling in the Washington-Baltimore Area

John Pescatore

EPM Publications, Inc.
McLean, Virginia

Library of Congress Cataloging-in-Publication Data

Pescatore, John.
   Family bicycling in the Washington-Baltimore area/John
Pescatore.
      p. cm.
   ISBN 0-939009-72-2
   1. Bicycle touring—Washington Metropolitan Area—
Guidebooks.   2. Bicycle touring—Maryland—Baltimore
Region—Guidebooks.   3. Washington Metropolitan Area—
Guidebooks.   4. Baltimore Region (Md.)—
Guidebooks.   I. Title.
   GV1045.5.W2P47   1993
   796.'4'09753—dc20   93-26389
                                                          CIP

EPM Publications, Inc., 1003 Turkey Run Road
   McLean, VA 22101
Printed in the United States of America

Book, cover and map designs by Konetzka Design Group

Contents

"The bicycle was perhaps our strongest ally in winning young men away from public houses, because it afforded them a pleasure far more enduring, and an exhilaration as much more delightful as the natural is than the unnatural."

> From *How I Learned to Ride the Bicycle—Reflections of an Influential 19th Century Woman* by Frances E. Willard, first published in 1895

"The bicycle...has been responsible for more movement in manners and morals than anything since Charles the Second. Under its influence, wholly or in part, have wilted chaperons, long and narrow skirts, tight corsets, hair that would come down, black stockings, thick ankles, large hats, prudery and fear of the dark; under its influence, wholly or in part, have bloomed weekends, strong nerves, strong legs, strong language, knickers, knowledge of make and shape, knowledge of woods and pastures, equality of sex, good digestion and professional occupation—in four words, the emancipation of women."

> John Galsworthy, as quoted in *How I Learned to Ride the Bicycle—Reflections of an Influential 19th Century Woman*

Introduction

The baby finally sleeps through the night. Sleep patterns are returning to normal, and there is a hint of spring in the air. Remember back before the baby, when the two of you would throw the bicycles on the car and spend the day cycling throughout the District? Does it now seem as if the only time you think of cycling is when you trip over those dusty ten-speeds on your way to dropping several hundred baby food jars into the recycling bin?

Perhaps you never were much of a bike rider, but now your children are old enough to ride two wheelers and they would like Mom and Dad to go riding with them. The only time you've touched a bike in fifteen years has been to put the kids' bikes together at midnight on Christmas Eve. Maybe it has been even longer than that; you are retired and are thinking about bicycling for exercise. From what you can remember about adult bicycles, they have these ridiculous drop handlebars and incredibly uncomfortable seats.

Maybe you are or will be vacationing in the Baltimore-Washington area and would like a day of family exercise to work off those crabcakes and ice cream. Your children are getting a little antsy with nothing more strenuous than shuffling through museums to burn off that excess energy.

Bicycling as a family activity has come a long way. Safer, easier to use kiddie seats, lightweight trailers, and hybrid bicycles for adults make bicycling today ideal for safe, healthy family exercise. In the Baltimore-Washington area, the popularity of cycling has lead to the development of an impressive network of bicycle paths and trails, providing hundreds of miles of scenic and safe bicycling routes. Whether your children are infants, grade schoolers or teenagers, a family bike ride is a great way to spend the day. For families just visiting this area, renting bikes and seeing the sites at a leisurely pace can be a memorable part of your vacation.

This book is a guide to great places for families to cycle in the Baltimore-Washington region. There are other cycling guidebooks for this area, but they concentrate on challenging rides that often climb mountains, or share the road with automobiles, or that are 60 or 100 miles in length. This book is oriented towards those of us who would feel silly wearing those Lycra shorts and aren't willing to take our kids out onto Route 1. (Of course, if you start cycling with your kids now, you might look good in those tights by the time the kids hit college.)

The routes detailed in this book will be attractive to families and us middle-of-the-road cyclists. They are generally level, are off the road on paths, or are on roads with wide, smooth shoulders. They also include attractions such as playgrounds, lakes or parks to make a day trip worthwhile. I have ridden all of these routes with my 12-year-old son and 2-year-old daughter, but I also ride them on those rare occasions where I can get out by myself. These are fun places to ride at a leisurely pace with your children, or on a clear spring day with your significant other, or at a brisk pace as you go for some aerobic exercise. By the way, the same qualities that make these routes attractive for cycling with children (flat, paved, off-the-street, scenic) also make them ideal for in-line skating or cross-country skiing.

The first several sections of the book are oriented toward getting started in cycling with your family: how to select the right bicycles and other equipment, how to teach your children to ride and to ride safely, and how to transport riders and equipment to the good places to ride. The heart of the book is the Routes section, which provides descriptions of 37 great family rides, along with detailed directions and guides to points of interest. The Resource section provides information on how to expand these routes into longer, more challenging rides, as well as phone numbers for the many organizations in the Baltimore-Washington area dedicated to advancing the cause of cycling in this region.

There are so many great places to ride bicycles in Maryland, the District and Virginia that the hard part of writing the book was deciding what to leave out. Most of the rides listed are within an hour's drive of Baltimore or Washington (a few that are farther away were too good to leave out). Many of them may be within blocks of where you live. Get out there with your kids, your spouse or even your grandmother and try a few of these routes. See turtles sunning on rocks in the C&O Canal. Show your children deer bounding through the fields that surround the Northern Central Rail Trail. Pedal underneath the Beltway and sneer at all the motorists grinding their teeth, sucking in exhaust fumes. Look for Carole and me, pulling Lauren and trying to keep up with Kevin.

J.P.

Equipment

If you already have a bicycle, get out there and ride! If you are planning to buy a bike for yourself or your children, spend a little time and make sure you get one that is right for you. Just as ill-fitting shoes can turn a pleasurable hike into a nightmare, the wrong bicycle or equipment can take all the fun out of an enjoyable ride.

Bicycles

There have been many changes in bicycle technology over the last five years. In the good old days it was simple: kids went from tricycles to banana seats and butterfly handlebars to ten-speeds. Adults usually rode three-speeds or maybe ten-speeds. Today the array of choices may seem bewildering, but if you strip away fad-driven issues, choosing a bike is still fairly straightforward.

Children can start pedaling tricycles and small two-wheelers with training wheels as early as two years of age. Since they won't put a lot of mileage on these starter bikes before they outgrow them, there is no reason not to buy one of the more inexpensive models sold at toy and department stores. But for older children and adults, the money spent buying a slightly more expensive bicycle at a bicycle shop will more than pay off over the years.There is nothing more frustrating than trying to adjust or repair a cheaply made kid's bike—and they will require a lot of both.

Two-Wheelers for Children. For children in the four- to five-year-old range, the typical starter bike will have 16-inch wheels, no gears, coaster (foot-powered) brakes and removable training wheels. Some of these bicycles will have a hand-operated brake that slows the front wheel while the foot brake operates on the rear wheel. Younger children tend not to use the hand brakes, which is just as well. Using only the front brake to stop a bike traveling at a high speed can cause the child to flip over the handlebars. The bike should come with front and rear reflectors and reflectors in the wheel spokes. The seats on these bikes tend to be hard plastic and very uncomfortable, but at this age not enough time is spent actually sitting on the seat to make it a problem.

Selecting a bike that fits your child is very important. Make sure that the balls of the child's feet can touch the ground when he is straddling the bike. If you will initially be using training wheels, you can use a slightly bigger bike for your child to grow into as long as the child's feet can firmly reach the pedals at their lowest position. The block-like attachments that go on pedals to let a child use a bigger bicycle are not very useful. Buy a smaller bike. Check that the child's arms are long enough to securely reach the handlebars when the child is sitting on the bicycle seat. A decent bike in this category will range from $120 to $250 and will last most children until they are eight to ten years old. Less expensive bikes are available, but they will not last as long and they will require almost constant adjustment and maintenance.

Older children, or those who have outgrown these smaller bikes, can start on 20-inch single-speed bikes, perhaps one with coaster brakes and a hand-operated front brake. There is really no need for multiple speeds for this size bike. The small frame sizes of these bikes make gear-changing systems very unreliable, and the beating that a bicycle takes from a 10 or 12 year old takes its toll on components. Children of this age will not be riding up long, steep hills anyway, but the fad has been for all bikes to have at least five or six speeds. These BMX (bicycle motocross) style bikes will last many kids until they are 12 to 14 years old, or children with longer legs may graduate to a 24-inch bike. But with the popularity of 26-inch mountain bikes, there is usually no reason to buy a 24-inch bike. Look for a bike with 26-inch wheels and a small frame. By lowering the seat and the handlebars, you can buy a bike that will last your child for the next ten years. The same principles apply for sizing bicycles in this category: Make sure your child can comfortably straddle the frame and reach the handlebars when seated. The bicycle shop will adjust the seat and handlebar heights to match your child's size. These bikes range from $175 to $350.

Since these days few girls will be riding a bike while wearing a long skirt, there is really no reason to get a "girl's bike"— one with a slanted bar connecting the seat post and the neck of the handlebars. There is no reason not to, however, if your daughter wants one. The frames will stand up to the same level of use as will the standard bicycle frame. The decision is essentially a fashion issue; there is no safety-related reason why a girl should not ride a boy's bike.

Parents' Bikes. The fastest-selling types of bicycles sold today are mountain bikes and hybrid, or fitness, bikes. Mountain bikes have fat, stubby tires, straight handlebars and very rugged frames. Fittingly, they are designed to withstand being ridden down mountains, over logs and through streams. Unless you are planning on taking your children on some breathtaking rides, mountain bikes are generally heavier and more expensive than you will need. However, mountain biking can be a lot of fun—when you are in the mountains. For now, let's concentrate on a bike to ride in your neighborhood or on the paths and trails described in this book.

For general purpose biking, a hybrid bicycle is intended for casual riders (not racers) who want a balance between comfort, ruggedness and speed. These bikes generally have soft, gel-filled seats, upright handlebars, and medium-width tires that combine for a very comfortable ride. They are also called fitness bikes since they are often the choice of those who want to ride a bicycle for aerobic exercise or weight loss but who don't plan on entering the Tour de France. The frames and wheels are sturdier than road or racing bikes, and there are usually attachment points (called braze-ons) for things like racks and water bottles.

Almost any adult bicycle these days has a minimum of 21 speeds. You may only use three or four, but it is near impossible to find an adult bicycle with fewer than 12 speeds. Those extra gears may come in handy if you are pulling a kiddie trailer over even a modestly hilly route. All new bikes use indexed gear shifting, which means you simply move a lever until it clicks, and the bike automatically shifts one gear up or down.

Hybrid bicycles from major manufacturers such as Raleigh, Schwinn, Mongoose or Trek can be found over a wide range of prices. For a bike that will be sturdy yet lightweight and reliable, $300 is about the bottom level. Look for sales before Christmas or in the early spring, as dealers try to make room for the next year's models. Sizing a bike for adults is similar to doing so for children: Choose a frame size that lets you straddle the bike with both feet firmly on the ground. The bike shop will adjust the seat and handlebar height to fit your torso size. Sizing for women is a little different than for men, since women are generally not as tall as men and have shorter arms. The basic rules for selecting the right size frame still apply, but the seat height and handlebar position will need to adjusted differently than for a man.

One hint about adjusting your bicycle seat: Many people find it much more comfortable riding with the seat tilted slightly down in front. This places more pressure on the bottom than on the pelvic bone, eliminating that numbness that creeps in after a long ride. Don't tilt the seat too far forward; this will shift too much weight onto your arms and lead to sore shoulders, arms and hands.

If you still have a dusty old three-speed cruiser in the garage, dust it off and try it out. Many of the best family cycling spots in the Baltimore-Washington area are nearly table-top flat, and that old balloon-tire job will probably do the trick. A good bicycle can make a real difference, however. Climbing that last hill on the way to Mount Vernon can be a real grind on a clunker; shift your new hybrid into low gear and you will barely notice it.

Tandems. The old bicycle built for two is making a comeback. Though they are certainly not cheap—$1,000 is about the lower limit—tandems are the perfect way for two people of unequal cycling ability to enjoy a bike ride together. Tandems have two seats, two sets of handlebars and two sets of pedals. The rider in the front is called the captain and gets to steer, shift and brake. The rider in the back is called the stoker and basically just pedals and looks around, or sometimes just looks around if the captain doesn't notice. There are even triples, which include a midshipman for more pedalling power.

If you are frustrated trying to ride with a spouse or child who rides much more slowly than you do, a tandem might be just the thing for you. Children's stoker kits are available that raise the rear set of pedals high enough for even a five year old to ride safely and comfortably. Most tandems can also hold a kiddie seat or pull a trailer, although you should become very comfortable riding a tandem before you put on a kiddie seat. Some tandems have drum brakes in the rear that interfere with a trailer-mounting hitch. Tandems are available in road, hybrid or mountain bike models.

Tandems are long and heavy, but they are still smaller and lighter than two individual bikes. Several bike shops in this area, such as Monkton Bike Rental on the NCRR trail, Pedal Pushers on the Baltimore Annapolis trail, Thompson's Boat Center at the Georgetown end of the C&O Canal, and Mount Airy Bicycles, will rent tandems for you to try out.

Child Carriers and Trailers

Our first family cycling outing was an enjoyable ride on the Youghiogheny River Trail in Pennsylvania when my daughter Lauren was ten months old. If your child is old enough to sit upright unsupported, she is old enough to go with you on a bicycle ride. Generally, by the time they are eight to ten months old, babies have developed strong enough neck muscles to hold up their heads and a lightweight helmet long enough for an enjoyable ride. If you are unsure about your child's development, check with your pediatrician before riding. Any child of any age should *always* wear a helmet when cycling.

The least expensive way to bring your infant along is to use a bicycle kiddie seat that mounts above the rear wheel of your bicycle. Kiddie seats range in price from $30 to $120 and are easily installed with common tools. These seats are relatively inexpensive, lightweight and are generally safe. However, they do drastically affect the ride and handling of your bicycle. Your child's weight is placed high above the ground and near the rear of your bike, requiring you to be careful in turning, stopping and dismounting. Kiddie seats also do not provide full protection in the event of a serious crash. A child wearing a helmet in a well-designed kiddie seat is protected from serious injury, but the child's arms and legs are still exposed to bruises and abrasions.

The minimum features to look for in a kiddie seat are:

- Leg shields. These plastic shields ensure that your child's legs cannot come in contact with the rear wheel. They also provide additional protection if the bicycle should fall over.
- Five-point harness. A simple lap belt is neither secure enough protection in a crash nor devious enough to thwart active squirmers. Look for a five-point harness with straps that go around the waist, over the shoulders and between the legs.
- A removable, washable pad. It can be bumpy back there. A pad is a must to help cushion the ride. As a parent, you probably already know why it should be removable and washable.

Some kiddie seats offer reclining seat backs, which can come in handy for inducing sleep in cranky little passengers. A nice feature on some of the more expensive seats is a mounting system that allows you to move the seat between different bicycles (if you buy additional mounting racks) or quickly remove the seat when you are riding without children.

An old way of carrying a passenger on a bike has become safer and more popular. EuroSeat and SAFE-T Cycling make child carrier seats that mount on the horizontal tube of your bicycle frame, between the seat and the handlebar stem. The SAFE-T Cycling Companion Carrier has foot rests that also mount on the bike frame, and the child balances on the seat and holds onto the handlebars. The EuroSeat also mounts to the horizontal tube but the seat is more like a highchair seat, with legholes and sides. While both of these look awkward, they keep the child enclosed within your arms and gives her an unobstructed view looking forward.

Our initial ride with Lauren convinced me a kiddie seat of either design was not the long-term solution for us. The bicycle felt very awkward with Lauren's weight up so high, and there was no easy way to give her access to toys or snacks. Her face was also vulnerable to low-hanging branches and oncoming bees. In the last five years a number of companies have introduced lightweight bicycle trailers for pulling children along behind your bike. Trailers have many advantages in safety, comfort and ease of use, but they are not cheap. The least expensive trailer is the Kiddie Kart marketed by several companies. It has a high-impact plastic shell and carries two children facing backwards. With a seat pad and fabric sun cover, this trailer is available in the $200 range.

The Kiddie Kart attaches to the seat post of your bicycle, which does affect the handling of your bicycle and makes pulling the trailer very noticeable. Since the children sit on a shell with no frame above, tipping over can be extremely dangerous. The hitch on the Kiddie Kart is designed to let the trailer remain upright, however, even if the bicycle falls. The plastic shell is also very noisy when ridden on gravel or dirt paths. This trailer is widely used, though, and with a little care is extremely safe.

Several companies make trailers with aluminum and steel frames and nylon sides and covers that provide full protection, at a higher cost. The Burley and Equinox models have aluminum frames enclosed in tentlike fabric and hold two children facing forward. The trailer attaches to the bicycle frame near the rear wheel and has almost no effect on the handling of your bicycle. The mounting bracket also swivels, allowing the trailer to stay upright even if the bicycle should fall over. The Burley and Equinox models have child-accessible side pockets for storing toys or Cheerios, and rear storage that the kids cannot reach. With covers, these trailers run in the $250 to $350 range.

Winchester makes a steel-framed trailer with nylon sides and a unique combination cover that allows you to choose clear plastic or nylon mesh covers, depending on weather conditions. Two children can ride in the Winchester trailer, with one facing forward and one facing backward. This split seating arrangement keeps some space between little fists and feet or can be used to change a single child's seating position to keep the sun out of those sensitive eyes. The seats can also be individually set to a reclining position. The mounting arrangement is similar to the Burley/Equinox, with excellent handling and stability. The steel frame and five-point hitch seat straps make this one of the safest trailers available. The Winchester is available in the $300 to $350 range.

Blue Sky was one of the earliest manufacturers of cycling trailers, and they still make some of the most innovative designs around. They sell the only trailer built to carry four children, and they have a version that will even carry a wheelchair. I hesitate to even bring it up, but a number of people use Blue Sky trailers to bring dogs—large dogs—along when they cycle.

CycleTote trailers use bicycle wheels for a smooth, low-friction ride, and the Family Model is a very well put together children's trailer. Even though the hitch attaches to the seat post, the trailer stays upright no matter what happens to the bicycle. CycleTote also has an optional automatic braking system, which applies drum brakes to the trailer wheels when the bicycle begins to brake. This can be a big help going down steep hills or when pulling a trailer behind a tandem. The CycleTote trailers fold into a compact package.

Many of these trailers fold up to fit in some automobile trunks and come with orange pennants on a detachable mast to increase visibility. Bicycle trailers are becoming extremely popular, and several other companies such as CycleTote and Cannondale have new products coming out. All the trailers discussed above are available from many local bicycle shops, with Mount Airy Bicycles having the widest selection, or by mail order from outfits such as Nashbar and Colorado Cyclist. A few bicycle shops rent trailers by the hour, so you can try one out before you buy. To take infants along, many people actually put the child's car seat in the trailer and buckle it in.

Another new concept is the Adams Trail-A-Bike, which is kind of like a small bicycle with no front wheel that attaches to the seat post of your bicycle and trails behind your rear wheel. It looks like a third wheel attached to your bike, with a seat and pedals for a child to ride. The Trail-A-Bike is geared such that the child actively pedals up to about 12 miles per hour but can coast whenever she gets tired. Since the child must balance on the seat, this arrangement is for kids between four and ten who can ride a bike but not fast enough to keep up with grownups. The Trail-A-Bike is a much more aerodynamic way of riding than pulling a trailer. Adams also has a version for handicapped children that allows the child to be strapped into the seat and securely supported. The Trail-A-Bike sells in the $250 range.

Pulling a trailer is surprisingly easy on level ground. On hills, the added weight (an empty trailer weighs anywhere from 19 to 27 pounds) becomes painfully obvious; if you are not ready for the Tour de France, you should stick to level ground when pulling a trailer. On level ground you should be able to average seven to ten miles per hour. An hour of steady riding is perfect for both aerobic benefit and most babies' tolerance level. We have found that a 20- to 25-mile round trip, with a long break in the middle, makes for a pleasant morning or afternoon ride. If Mom or Dad is a much stronger cyclist than the other, pulling a trailer is a great equalizer. I pull Lauren (now two years old) in the Winchester trailer and one hour seems to be her tolerance limit. If we are foolish enough to try riding for longer than an hour without stopping, Lauren lets us know in no uncertain terms that it is time to take a break! Scheduling the ride so that the return trip hits right at Lauren's usual nap time works well; before Lauren can gather the energy to start screaming, she falls asleep.

Helmets

Everyone should wear a helmet when cycling. Three-quarters of the 1,000 or so deaths from bicycling crashes each year are due to head injuries. Scrapes and bruises will heal; cracked skulls often will not. Helmets help motorists see you more easily, but the main purpose is to protect your brain from any sudden impact. A bicycle helmet reduces the peak energy that reaches your head when it is struck by a hard surface, much like an airbag reduces the impact of a car crash. To do this requires a layer of stiff foam that crushes under impact and dissipates the force before it reaches your noggin. Most helmets use a substance called EPS for this layer, the same white material that picnic coolers are made from. There are also two types of outer surfaces on helmets, called hard shells and soft shells. The hard shell helmets cover the EPS foam with a plastic shell to help spread impact energy. These helmets will take a little more abuse and may be a little safer. Soft shell helmets are a bit lighter and may be a better choice for babies. There is not really much difference. It is important that the helmet stay on your head during impact, so all good helmets will have D rings or a high-quality, adjustable strap and buckle arrangement.

How do you know if a helmet is designed well enough to protect you or your children? There are two standards in the U.S. for bicycle helmets. The best helmets meet the Snell Memorial Foundation standard; others should at least meet the ANSI standard. The helmet should have a sticker on the inside stating which standards it meets. The May 1990 issue of Consumer Reports had a detailed comparison of bicycle helmets, or you can contact the Bicycle Helmet Safety Institute at 703-486-0100 for more information.

Most helmets come with various sizes of foam pads that allow you to fit the helmet to your or your child's head. Try and find a helmet that fits well with the smallest possible pads. Helmets should sit on top of the head in a level position and not rock back and forth or sideways. Bald parents and babies should avoid helmets with large air vents on top, unless you enjoy stripes of sunburn across your head. A good helmet will cost from $25 to $50.

Accessories

If you like accessorizing, bicycling is the sport for you. You could easily spend more on clothes and doo-dads than you did on the bicycles. You don't need to buy much, though; a few essential items and you are set for an enjoyable ride.

A small tool pouch to carry on your bike is a must. Tool "wedges" that mount under your seat are handy for carrying pliers, tire patch kits, tire pressure gauges, and other tools for simple repairs. I think all adult bikes should have a rear rack that is not only convenient for carrying things but also acts as a shield between your back and the mud that can be thrown upwards from your rear wheel. A frame-mounted pump is also nice to have, since fixing a flat is a waste of time if you can't pump up the newly repaired tire. Be sure to get a pump that handles both Schrader (the same valve as in your car tire) and Presta valves, since kids' bikes tend to have Schrader valves and adults' bikes (the newer ones any-way) come with the narrower Presta valves.

A sturdy lock is also important. More bicycles than cars are stolen each year, so be sure to lock all your bikes. For locking one bike at a time, U-shaped steel locks are reliable and easy to carry, but they don't work very well for multiple bikes or trailers. Since on most family rides you won't be leaving your bikes alone for long periods of time, a well-de-signed cable lock is probably sufficient. If you already have some chain and a padlock and don't mind carrying the extra weight, by all means use that.

For most family riding, sneakers are the footwear of choice. For some reason, the latest generation of bikes has es-chewed the use of chain guards, so keep the laces on every-body's right foot short and to the right side of the sneaker. Getting a lace caught in the chain can cause some interesting crashes. If you find you are doing a lot of cycling, you may want to try a pair of cycling shoes and a set of toe clips. Cycling shoes have stiffer soles than standard sneakers, which helps distribute the pressure of the pedals across your feet; the difference is noticeable. You can get them on sale at many bike shops for a bit more than regular sneakers. Toe clips keep your feet centered on the pedals and help you pull up on the upstroke. Once you get the hang of them, it is easy to get your feet in or out, but make sure you are com-fortable using toe clips before your try them with a child on your bike. Children should be experienced cyclists before they try toe clips.

Cycling gloves look odd but can help ease the pressure of the handlebars on your palms. I wouldn't spend any money on cycling jerseys or those stretchy cycling pants. There really are advantages to them for serious cyclists, but I would feel silly walking around in them and I don't think my kids would want to be seen anywhere near me. A good pair of shorts in the summer and sweatpants or jeans in cooler weather work just fine. On the other hand, cycling pants do have built-in padding which can help avoid cy-cling's most common ailment—the sore bottom syndrome. If you have a relatively new bicycle it will have a gel-filled seat, that will go a long way towards reducing discomfort. For older bicycles, most bike shops sell padded seat covers that perform the same function.

One of the more useful technological advances in cycling accessories has been inexpensive trip computers. These little digital readouts mount on your handlebars and have sensors that read the turns of your wheels and pedals. Trip computers read out distance, speed, average speed, and pedal cadence. There are also models that will tell you the altitude and how high you have climbed! All of the routes described in this book have mileage markings taken from my bicycle trip computer. Keeping track of how far you have ridden is a good way to gauge your family's tolerance for long rides, and plotting your total mileage on a chart or on your home computer gives children a real sense of accomplishment. Trip computers run from $20 to $60. If you buy one at a local bike shop they will usually install it for free.

The slightly more expensive cycling computers will display cadence, or the number of times you pedal each minute. This is a nice feature for beginning riders of multigear bicycles, who have a tendency to use too high a gear and pedal at too slow a rate. This puts undue stress on your knees, causes lactic acid to build up more quickly, and is generally fatiguing. You should try to always use a gear that lets you pedal comfortably at a 70–80 pedals per minute rate. At this rate you should be able to maintain 10 to 15 miles per hour, burning 30 to 40 calories for each mile you ride.

One of the most useful and least expensive accessories is a frame-mounted water bottle. For less than five dollars you can get a plastic water bottle and a bracket that mounts to braze-ons (welded-on threaded connectors) on the frame of your bike. While most of the rides in this book have water fountains or grocery stores nearby, it is always a good idea to carry water when you ride. The breeze you create by cycling evaporates perspiration very quickly, and you can easily become dehydrated. Try to find a water bottle with a neck wide enough to fit standard sized ice cubes—a nice way to beat the heat during our muggy summers.

There are a wide variety of rack- and handlebar-mounted bags you can buy that are nice for carrying snacks, toys, tissues or first aid kits. Sponge handlebar grips are good to absorb sweat and reduce the impact of bumps. Many of the newer bikes come with these, but they are easy to install if yours did not.

Learning to Ride

A bicyclist of any age (even infants riding in trailers) should always wear a helmet. It is important to make putting on a helmet as natural as putting on shoes. The best way to ensure that your children wear their helmets is for you to wear your helmet. Make it one of those adult rituals that children love to imitate, like shaving or wearing a bra. If you will be riding with grade-school age children, your biggest problem will probably be keeping up with them! Children can start riding two-wheel bicycles with training wheels when they are still preschoolers. When they are familiar with the basics of turning, stopping, and getting on and off the bike, most kids are ready to learn to ride without training wheels.

The safest and simplest way to help your child learn to ride a two-wheeler is to find a smooth grassy area with a gradual slope. Tell your child that you don't expect everything to click the first time and that there is nothing to be ashamed of if he falls a few times. Take your time and if your child gets frustrated, take a break. Remove the training wheels from the bicycle and make sure that the seat is low enough for your child's feet to just touch the ground. Have your child coast down the hill, with his feet off the pedals, until he is comfortable maintaining his balance. If necessary, let your child scoot his feet on the ground the first time or two, just to get the hang of it. You may have to run along next to the bike the first few times, but minimize this so that your child will develop confidence along with balance.

When coasting has been mastered, raise the seat to where your child's knees remain slightly bent when the pedal is at the lowest point. If your child can't touch the ground with his feet, however, lower the seat a bit for now. Have your child start pedaling slowly as he gets moving down a gradual grade. The hardest part to master is getting started, so hold on to the back of the seat the first few times if your child is having difficulty. Have him brake to a stop a few times to master the brakes and stopping, and then start up again on his own. Stick with it; even though it may take a number of attempts, sooner or later your child will be pedalling like a pro. Take along your video camera for this initial solo outing; I wish I had recorded the look on my son Kevin's face when he realized I was no longer holding up the bike. If times runs out before this magic occurs, give your child some encouraging words and don't put those training wheels back on. Try again as soon as possible after the first session.

The final stage is to move to a safe, level, paved area such as a parking lot or cul de sac and practice starting from a standstill and stopping. A parking lot with painted lines is a good place to practice riding in a straight line. This will be a lot more fun if you can join in on your bike and play follow-the-leader. Take turns being the leader and before you know it your child will be riding circles around you.

Once your child has grown confident in balancing and stopping, try a short ride together in a park, stopping at the playground or pond. Let your child set the pace. Those little leg muscles can tire out, and when your child's concentration slips, spills and scrapes are more likely. When Kevin was seven, his energy was boundless but his legs and attention span were short. A ride at his pace might include a stop at the swings or the zoo, and short side excursions to investigate interesting areas.

Riding Safely

Although bicycling is not an inherently dangerous sport, there are a lot of serious cycling-related injuries each year. The statistics show that every day in the U.S. at least one child aged 14 or younger dies in a bicycle crash. Head injuries cause three out of four of these deaths and most of the serious injuries as well. A common misconception is that these deaths and serious injuries only occur when kids ride into the street and are hit by a car. Most injuries, and almost one-fifth of all fatal accidents, occur when a cyclist simply runs into a stationary object, like a tree or pothole, without wearing a helmet.

The most important considerations for safe cycling are:
• Everyone should always wear a helmet.
• Everyone should understand the basics of bicycle safety.
• Make sure your child's bike is selected and adjusted to meet his or her size and abilities.
• Stay off the roads until you are very confident in your child's ability and safety consciousness.

In order to increase the odds that your children do not become part of these depressing statistics, go over these basics with them before letting them ride on their own. By following these four simple rules, you and your children can avoid the most common types of cycling injuries:

1. A bicyclist has to obey all the same road signs that someone driving a car has to obey. This includes stop signs, traffic lights, pavement markings and yield signs.
2. Bicyclists should always ride with the flow of traffic and stay as far to the right as possible. For years there has been urban folklore that it is safer to ride into traffic, I guess so that you can see the traffic. However, it is much safer to ride in the direction that motorists expect to find traffic; the better view is not worth the greatly increased danger.

3. Always look for traffic in front of you and behind you before making a turn. As a motorist you know that you have blind spots in your rear- and side-view mirrors that can hide a car. A small child on a bicycle is even easier to miss. This is especially critical when a cyclist is making a left turn.
4. Always, always, always, stop and check both ways for traffic before riding out onto a road. More than half of fatal accidents occur when a child rides out into traffic without stopping to check for danger.

Most of the routes in this book are on bicycle trails and involve little or no cycling on roadways. While there is no danger of being hit by a car on a bicycle trail, in some ways you need to be even more safety conscious on these trails. On many trails there will be a mixture of cyclists, joggers, walkers, dogs, strollers and even horses. On most trails, cyclists must yield the right of way to horses and pedestrians. When overtaking slower traffic, always pass on the left and give some kind of audible warning. Most trails require some kind of horn or bell on every bicycle for this purpose. A common, and sensible, practice is to loudly say "On your left!" 15 to 20 feet before passing. Slow down, and keep your hands on the brakes as you go by.

Another common danger on bicycle paths are wet leaves. Most of the paths described here go through wooded areas, and from October through March they are often covered with leaves. After rainfall these leaves are doubly treacherous: The wet surface of the leaves is slippery, and the leaves themselves will also skid on the asphalt path. In mapping out one of the routes in Rock Creek Park, I tried to pass someone on a curvy section of the trail that was covered with wet leaves. I had a painful, and embarrassing, wipeout that left my knees and elbows covered with scrapes. Whenever you see leaves, slow down and ride as straightly as possible. On steep downhill sections, walk your bikes until the slope of the hill has leveled out.

Many schools have bicycle education programs that really help to burn these lessons in. Ask your school system or contact the League of American Wheelmen or the National Safe Kids campaign, listed in the Resource section.

Getting It All There

Some of the places to ride listed in the Routes section will be close enough to your house that you and your family can simply hop on the bikes at your house and ride right to the trail or park. When this is not the case, you always have the problem of how to get everyone and their bicycles there and back. Fortunately, the popularity of bicycling has lead manufacturers to introduce a number of solutions to this problem.

The most common way of carrying bicycles on a car is the trunk rack. This works best when there are no more than two or three bicycles to carry and when your car is a standard sedan with a trunk. The rack has clips that hook under the trunk lid, and padded feet to keep from scratching your car. The bikes rest on padded arms, either horizontally or vertically, depending on the model. These racks are inexpensive and available at any bicycle shop. They do not easily hold trailers and don't work very well with some vans or hatchbacks.

If you have a trailer hitch on your vehicle, you can take advantage of a new way to carry bicycles. Trailer hitch mounts replace the ball on your trailer hitch with a vertical bike carrier, some of which can carry up to three bikes. Some of these carriers come with stabilization straps that clip to your car; some are made of very heavy duty metal and don't require these straps. I used one of these to carry three bikes to Deep Creek Lake and it worked great. These are slightly more expensive than trunk racks.

If you have a pickup truck, you can simply lay the bikes down in the pickup bed, but this will scratch and damage the bikes and it can be difficult to untangle the bikes after a bumpy trip. Most bike shops sell bars with quick-release wheel attachment devices that mount across the bed using clamps or friction mounts. You remove the front wheel of each bicycle and attach the fork to the quick-release mount.

The bike stays vertical and you can fit four bicycles in a small truck and five or six in a full-size pickup.

The most expensive, but increasingly popular, racks are roof racks. These are available for a wide variety of cars and look like the roof-mount ski racks that have been around for years. These use quick-release arrangements similar to the pickup track mount, and the bicycle stands vertically on the roof of your car. It is possible to hold four bicycles on large cars, and by using tie-down straps you can even carry a trailer up there. It is a little tricky getting the bikes up there, especially on a van or large car, but it is a very convenient way to carry bikes without obstructing access to the trunk of your car. One danger is forgetting that the bikes are up there and driving into a garage or under other low-hanging obstacles. Several hundred dollars of bicycle and rack can be quickly removed from your car that way. For short trips, such as many in this book, roof racks are probably overkill, unless you ski a lot as well. If you intend to bring bikes on vacation or to some of the more remote rides described here, these racks are a good investment.

Route Index and Overview Map

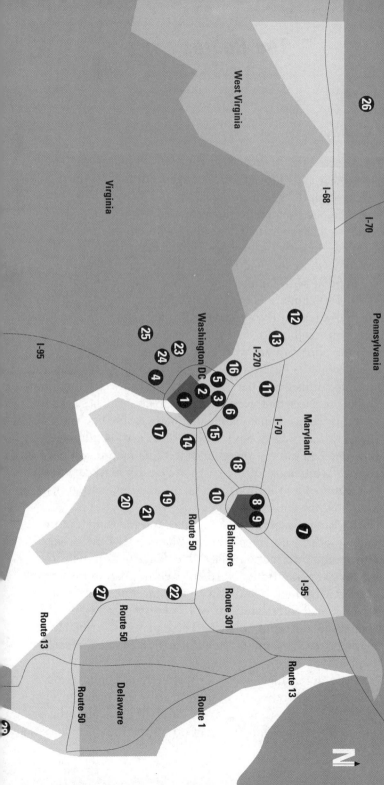

Overview Map

West Virginia

Virginia

Pennsylvania

Maryland

Washington DC

Baltimore

Delaware

I-68

I-70

I-70

I-270

I-95

I-95

Route 50

Route 50

Route 50

Route 301

Route 13

Route 13

Route 1

N

26
12
13
25
23
24
4
16
5
2
3
1
6
11
15
17
14
18
10
8
9
7
20
19
21
27
22

The Routes

I've selected the following 37 routes from places my family has ridden and enjoyed. They range from four to thirty miles in length, with options to lengthen and shorten most rides. I've included pointers to playgrounds, rest rooms and parks—all the essentials for riding with children. These routes are mostly on bicycle or hiker/biker paths, but there are some short on-road stretches on several of the rides. All are popular with families and older cyclists, who are not looking to climb hills or challenge tractor trailer trucks on the highways. At the end of the Routes listing are some future trails to look for and some places that didn't make it into the book but are worth mentioning.

Each ride listing begins with a description of the ride and some local history. There are directions to the starting point and a cue sheet that gives detailed directions. These are followed by maps. Some people like maps, some like cue sheets. I like to have both, since I often get lost no matter how detailed the cue sheets and need the map to get back on course. While most of the paths are clearly marked (except in Columbia and Reston), the maps are a big help in planning how far you want to go.

The Resource section lists sources for additional, more detailed maps from which you can plan longer rides or get more route information. There are detailed strip maps out for the three rail trails (Northern Central, Baltimore Annapolis, and Washington and Old Dominion Rail Trails) that provide detailed directions, lots of local history, and information about surrounding areas. These maps are available at many bookstores and at the information centers on each of the trails.

If you are a single parent or just hesitant about trying some of these routes on your own, there are several cycling clubs that sponsor group family rides. In particular, the Baltimore Bicycling Club has spun off a group for people riding with children. Each year the group plans several rides to places listed in this book, as well as other weekend-long rides. We rode with them on a group ride on the Baltimore Annapolis Rail Trail and had a blast. Contact Ken Greco at 301-381-0768. There is also a new cycling club for senior citizens being formed by Dr. Charles Miller, director of the Maryland Chiropractic Center in Clinton, Md. Plans for the club call for meeting a few mornings a week in a park or other off-road cycling spot for an hour of leisurely, social and beneficial pedalling. Contact Mary Farley of the Chiropractic Center at 301-868-1700 for information.

If your children's interest in cycling really takes off, the Bicycle Club of College Park has road and track racing programs for young cyclists. These programs are for children from eight to eighteen and are conducted by a United States Cycling Federation trained and licensed coach. In addition to individualized instruction, track bicycles and transportation from the College Park area to the Lehigh (Pennsylvania) County Velodrome are provided on a limited basis. Call Paul Bakos at 410-923-3135.

If you get tired of cycling on these routes, try in-line skating. On weekends at Quiet Waters and Rock Creek parks you are likely to see as many skaters as cyclists. If it snows, try cross-country skiing. These routes are flat, smooth, out of traffic and have many added attractions. Give them a try; if you know of, or discover, others, write and let me know.

Washington, DC Monuments Tour
7-mile loop

Every guide book to this area has to include a tour of the monuments in the District of Columbia, and for good reason. Riding a bicycle is cheaper than taking the Tourmobile and a lot better for you. There are paths and wide sidewalks for most of the trip, and you will get to see some things that might be obscured through the bus windows.

This seven-mile loop takes you around Haines Point, a man-made island across the Potomac from National Airport, where there is miniature golf, playgrounds and the dramatic statue called *The Awakening*. You will then head to the Jefferson Memorial perched on the edge of the Tidal Basin, where you can visit the memorial or rent paddle boats. Farther north is the Lincoln Memorial and then the Washington Monument. You can lock your bikes and walk east to the Smithsonian museums or the Capitol. There is no shortage of things to do in the Mall area, especially during the summer when there is some kind of festival almost every weekend.

I've included a swing by the Vietnam Veteran's Memorial, the newest and most dramatic structure on the Mall. Its sunken black stone design was initially controversial, but it has become one of the most heavily visited memorials in the District. To appease more traditional folks, a statue of soldiers and a flagpole was added at the southwest end of the memorial. Across Constitution Avenue from the Vietnam Veteran's Memorial is a 15-foot statue of Albert Einstein playing with the universe. This is a little off the beaten track but well worth the stop.

Start:
Ohio Drive, south of the Lincoln Memorial. Take the George Washington Parkway south from the Washington Beltway (I-495). Cross the Memorial Bridge, bear right and turn right at the first traffic light onto Ohio Drive. Park anywhere along the side of the street.

Miles	Directions
0.0	Head south on Ohio Drive. You can ride on the road or on the sidewalk that runs along the Potomac River. The road is quite rough.
0.5	Go over narrow bridge with the Jefferson Memorial to your left. Turn right after crossing bridge. You can continue on the road, or go across grass on your right to get back on the sidewalk.
1.1	Reach gate and Do Not Enter sign. Turn left on Buckeye Drive.
1.2	Turn right on Ohio Drive. You can stay on the road or get on the sidewalk.
2.3	Playground and rest rooms on left.
2.5	The statue *The Awakening* is straight ahead at the end of Haines Point. The statue is often under repair because astounded motorists tend to lose control and smash into it.
3.8	Continue around Haines Point, turn right at the gate at Buckeye Drive, which bisects the golf course.
3.9	This time turn *left* onto Ohio Drive. Miniature golf course on left.
4.3	Continue straight under bridge.
4.5	Bear right after going under bridge and cross 14th Street on crosswalk. The Jefferson Memorial is on your left via the sidewalk and is an impressive place to stop. There is a souvenir stand and rest rooms at the memorial. To continue tour, turn right on the sidewalk once you have crossed the street.

4.6   Immediately after crossing bridge, turn left from sidewalk onto path.

4.8   Reach boat rental area, where you can rent two- or four-seater paddle boats. There are also rest rooms and a snack bar.

5.0   Continue on path around Tidal Basin and walk bikes on narrow path over bridge.

5.2   Continue straight on sidewalk.

5.3   Turn right to cross Independence Avenue and get on opposite sidewalk. Turn right on sidewalk.

5.4   At 17th Street, turn left and follow sidewalk.

5.6   With the Lincoln Memorial on your left and the Washington Monument on your right, turn right on crosswalk at traffic light to cross 17th Street. Follow the path straight ahead to the Washington Monument.

5.8   Reach the Washington Monument, where your can lock bikes to go inside and up to the top of the monument. The Sylvan Theater is south of the monument, and there are concerts several days each week in the summer. Directly east are the Smithsonian museums and the Capitol building.

6.1   Head back towards the Lincoln Memorial on the same path and cross 17th Street at crosswalk at traffic light. Across street, bear right on the sidewalk and then turn left onto the path that leads to pond. Cross through open area and follow path to the right.

6.5   Continue around pond and turn right on path, away from pond, after passing entrance to a small island in the pond.

6.7 Reach east end of Vietnam Veterans Memorial. Bicycles are not allowed on the walkway that goes by the front of the memorial. You can lock your bikes to one of the streetlamps or fenceposts nearby.

6.8 West end of the memorial.

6.9 Continue around the Lincoln Memorial to Do Not Enter barricades, and turn left onto Ohio Drive towards traffic light. Continue on sidewalk to crosswalk and cross Independence to return to car.

Washington, DC Monuments Tour

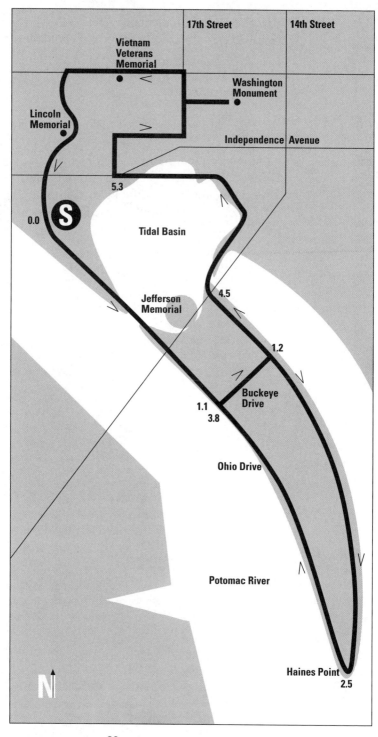

17th Street

14th Street

Vietnam Veterans Memorial

Washington Monument

Lincoln Memorial

Independence Avenue

5.3

0.0 **S**

Tidal Basin

Jefferson Memorial

4.5

1.2

Buckeye Drive

1.1
3.8

Ohio Drive

Potomac River

Haines Point
2.5

N

Rock Creek Park
13- and 17-mile tours

Rock Creek Park was created in 1890, and much like New York City's Central Park provides a refreshing greenway through the heart of urban territory. The Rock Creek Valley was originally settled by the Algonquin Indians and was later the site of many grist mills built and operated by European settlers. Over the years Rock Creek Park has been turned into a hiker and cyclist paradise, with sections of the main roadway (Beach Drive) closed to automobile traffic, a well-maintained asphalt path, and miles of hiking trails that are maintained by the Potomac Appalachian Trail Club.

The biking trail stretches 25 miles, from Lake Needwood in Rockville to the Memorial Bridge in Washington. The trail connects to the C&O Towpath and the Mount Vernon Trail; you could ride over 200 miles from Rockville to Cumberland, or 40 miles to Mount Vernon, and never be on a roadway. Each year the Potomac Area Council of the American Youth Hostels hosts the Capital Classic ride, which goes from Carter Barron Amphitheater to Haines Point and back, a 22-mile loop that attracts a crowd of over 4,000 cyclists including hundreds of children. After the ride there is a fair and a concert, and local restaurants donate breakfast and snacks. Contact the PAC-AYH at 202-783-4943 for details.

There are interesting sites along the entire path. The northern 13 miles in Maryland are the most rural and include an old railroad bridge, numerous parks and many stream crossings. Lake Needwood at the northern terminus has playgrounds, picnic areas, boat rentals and pontoon boat rides. South of the District line, you will pass by Fort De-Russey, which was built during the Civil War, and the Rock Creek Nature Center and Planetarium, where you can go on nature walks or take part in other ecology programs. Also at the Maryland border, just south of East West Highway, is the Rock Creek Park Horse Center, where you can go on trail rides or take riding lessons.

Farther south you will pass by the sites of several other Civil War forts as well as Pierce Mill, a restored grist mill where you can watch the water-powered millstones grind corn and wheat into fine flour. You can even take some flour home with you. The old carriage house behind the mill is now known as the Art Barn, a gallery where local artists display and sell their work. A few miles south of the mill you will reach the National Zoo, which is administered by the Smithsonian Institution. For years the zoo has been home to the perennially childless panda bears, Hsing-Hsing and Ling-Ling (Ling-Ling has passed away) as well as over 2,000 other animals. Admission to the zoo is free if you cycle in, and you can rent strollers or wagons once you get there.

If you are ambitious, you can ride the entire length of the trail, but I have found two favorite rides that our family likes to do that involve some cycling and a lot of other activities as well. The ride from Garrett Park to Lake Needwood is a 13-mile round trip, with parks and playgrounds at each end. The ride from Jones Mill to the zoo is a 17-mile round trip, but we usually spend an entire day at the zoo and the other interesting places to stop.

Continuing past the National Zoo past Georgetown to Gravelly Point is more urban cycling but provides the chance to watch planes land at National Airport or ride down to Haines Point to see the dramatic statue *The Awakening*. The two routes described below are just a sample of possible rides in Rock Creek Park.

Needwood Ride (13 miles)

Start:
Lake Needwood. Take Route 28 East from Rockville. Turn north on Avery Road. Turn left onto Needwood Lake Drive. At T, turn left and park at lakefront parking lot, or the larger parking lot farther down the road.

Miles	Directions
0.0	Begin at main parking lot adjacent to the boat rental area and snack bar. Follow park road south.

0.1 Turn right into the next parking lot, follow signs for hiker/biker trail. The trail starts out of the rear of the parking lot, to the left.

0.8 Cross Southlawn Road. Be careful of traffic, this can be a busy road.

1.1 Cross Avery Road.

1.3 There is a swinging bridge over the creek on your left.

1.8 Right before you go under the large overpass for Norbeck Road, a trail to your left will lead you to a shopping center and food area. Continue straight on main trail.

2.1 Cross Old Baltimore Road. Be careful: high speed traffic. There will be several side trails that lead off the main path. Continue straight.

3.6 Reach Aspen Hill Park, with ball fields and a water fountain. Turn around here for a seven-mile loop, or you can continue to Viers Mill Park for a nine-mile loop. If you continue, you will hit a few steep hills. To continue, go through the parking lot and turn right on Baltic. Immediately turn left on Adrian, and then cross Aspen Hill Road. Get on the sidewalk and turn right.

3.8 Cross Viers Mill Road at traffic light. Trail continues straight ahead.

4.1 Cross park road.

4.4 Cross park road.

4.5 Bear left on main path.

| 5.6 | Cross Randolph Road. Trail continues on right. |

| 6.6 | Pass through park and reach Viers Mill Park at Garrett Park Road. Retrace trail to return to Lake Needwood. |

National Zoo Loop (17 miles)

Start:

Take the Connecticut Avenue North exit from the Washington Beltway (I-495). Turn right at the traffic light onto Beach Drive. You can park at any of the parking areas along Beach Drive or continue south to the T with Stoneybrook Drive. Turn right onto Jones Mill Road and go under the Beltway. Park at any of the parking areas on the left side of the road for the next one-quarter of a mile.

Miles	Directions
0.0	Start at parking area along Stoneybrook Road or Jones Mill Road. Head south.
0.7	Cross bridge over stream.
0.9	Go under old railroad bridge. CAUTION: Trail gets narrow and steep under the bridge. Walk bikes or ride slowly and carefully.
1.3	Cross East West Highway after passing through park. Trail continues on the right side of the road along the stables. You can take horseback riding lessons or go on a trail ride at the stables.
1.6	Turn right after horse ring and follow signs to Candy Cane City playground.

1.8   Turn right to go over bridge opposite play-ground, at traffic light. There is no separate bike path for the next .7 miles, so you will be riding on the road. Since the road ahead is closed to vehicles on weekends, traffic is generally light, but be careful. If you want to shorten this loop and avoid this short stretch of road, you can park up ahead at the point where the road is shut off to cars.

2.5   Gates across road on weekends to keep out cars. This area is very popular with bikers and skaters and cross-country skiers in the winter. Since you have the entire road to yourself, it rarely feels crowded.

3.1   At Wise Road there is a short stretch where you share the roadway with cars. Stay to the right side of the road and continue straight along Beach Drive.

3.2   Car traffic exits to the right and bikers and hikers rule once more. There is some light auto traffic to the parking areas, however.

3.7   Road open to automobiles, ride on trail.

5.1   Cross road.

6.7   Cross road and head through parking lot directly ahead. Trail continues from rear of parking lot.

7.0   Reach Pierce Mill and Art Barn. On weekends you can grind corn into cornmeal at the mill. Water fountains and rest rooms available.

7.1   Cross bridge.

7.7   Bear left to cross bridge.

8.4 Reach main entrance to the National Zoo. Bicycle racks are located straight ahead. You can rent strollers and wagons for the little ones.

   South of the zoo, the bicycle path is clearly marked and easy to follow. About 2.3 miles south of the zoo you will reach the Georgetown end of the Chesapeake and Ohio Canal Towpath, which will take you through Georgetown and north along the Potomac River. If you continue south on the Rock Creek Trail, you will pass Thompson's Boat Center, where you can rent canoes, sailboats or tandem bikes, or watch the many college crew teams practice sculling on the river. About a mile and a half south of Georgetown you will reach the Lincoln Memorial, where you can connect to the Monuments Tour and Mount Vernon path rides described elsewhere in the book.

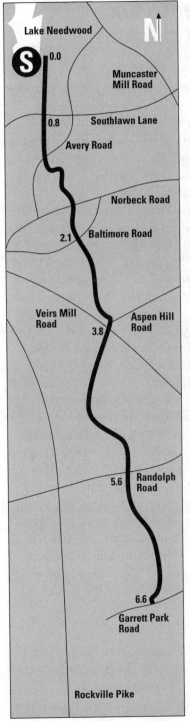

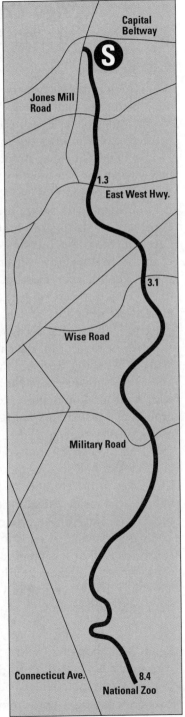

Rock Creek Park

Lake Needwood

S 0.0

Muncaster Mill Road

0.8 Southlawn Lane

Avery Road

Norbeck Road

2.1 Baltimore Road

Veirs Mill Road

Aspen Hill Road

3.8

Randolph Road

5.6

6.6

Garrett Park Road

Connecticut Ave.

Rockville Pike

N

Capital Beltway

S

Jones Mill Road

1.3 East West Hwy.

3.1

Wise Road

Military Road

8.4

National Zoo

Sligo Creek Park
10- and 3-mile tours

If you look in the dictionary under Family Cycling, you will
see a picture of Sligo Creek Park. This is one of the many
stream valley parks in central Maryland, with the greatest
density of playgrounds per mile of any path in the Northern
Hemisphere. The Piney Branch Path is one of the oldest
bikeways in the Washington area, and while it looks its age
it is still a fine place to cycle with children.

From Kemp Mill south, the bike path passes a playground
every few hundred yards while continuing to criss-cross Sligo
Creek. There is a golf course and snack bar midway, and it
is not far to downtown Silver Spring and many eateries and
shops. The southern-most section of this ride is on roadway
that is closed to cars on weekends. While there are not many
attractions along this stretch, it is a pretty ride and a great
place to let beginning cyclists practice their road skills.

North of Kemp Mill the shorter, newer section of trail
leads to Wheaton Regional Park, a child's delight. This is
one of the showpieces in Montgomery County's park system,
with a carousel, miniature train, enormous modern playground and a small animal farm that has been closed recently (it may reopen). There are hiking and biking paths
that lead to nearby Brookside Gardens, with a conservatory
and acres of bulbs, roses, ponds and colorful foliage. You can
lock bikes at the entrance to Brookside Gardens; bikes are
not allowed inside. Adjacent to the conservatory is a nature
center with interpretive programs and interesting displays.
The path system also leads to an ice skating rink and tennis
courts, as well as a campground in the middle of the sub-
urbs. Wheaton Regional Park can be very crowded on warm
weekends, but by cycling in you will bypass the hassle of
finding a parking spot.

Start:
Kemp Mill Shopping Center, Wheaton, Md. Take Route 193
(University Boulevard) north from the Washington Beltway
(I-495). Cross Colesville Road (Route 29) and then Dennis
Avenue. Turn right onto Arcola Avenue. Turn left into Kemp

Mill Shopping Center and park at rear of shopping center parking lot. Wheaton Regional Park telephone is 301-946-7033. Sligo Creek Stream Valley Park telephone is 301-650-2600.

Piney Branch Path (10-mile tour)

Miles	Directions
0.0	From rear of Kemp Mill parking lot take asphalt path to main path. Turn left onto path (turning right goes to Wheaton Regional Park, see below).
0.3	Cross University Boulevard to path on west side of Sligo Creek Avenue.
1.1	Large playground adjacent to path.
1.2	Cross Dennis Avenue.
1.8	Cross Forest Glen, then go under Washington Beltway overpass.
2.5	Cross over creek on bridge.
3.4	Cross over creek on bridge, hard left immediately over bridge.
3.6	Cross Flower Avenue.
3.9	To stay on path, cross bridge (walk bikes up steps). The alternative is a short ride on Sligo Creek Parkway.
4.2	Arrive at Piney Branch Avenue, a busy road. On Sundays from 11 A.M. to 6 P.M., Sligo Creek Parkway is closed to automobiles from Piney Branch to Maple Avenue; on other days the ride ends here. For some odd reason, probably bureaucratic, there is no way for bikes to get around the gates that block

automobile traffic. Carry your bike over or push it under the gate.

4.8	Nice playground on right.
5.0	Reach Maple Avenue and the end of the automobile-free section. There is another playground a half mile further on, but there is no place to ride other than on the road.

Wheaton Regional Park Path (3-mile tour)

Miles	Directions
0.0	From rear of Kemp Mill parking lot take asphalt path to main path. Turn right onto path (turning left goes to Sligo Creek Park, see above).
0.4	Bear left on trail.
0.6	Asphalt path ends at Channing Drive; go straight onto Ventura Avenue. This is a quiet residential street and quite safe, but be careful—there are cars on this road.
0.8	Ventura ends at Nairn; turn right. Another quiet neighborhood street with very little traffic.
0.9	Cross Arcola—be careful, this is a busy street.
1.0	Enter Wheaton Regional Park and go straight on the asphalt trail.
1.2	Follow trail to parking lot near carousel and miniature train station. From here you can walk or ride to Brookside Gardens, the Nature Center or the lake. There are several maps posted showing the location of these attractions.

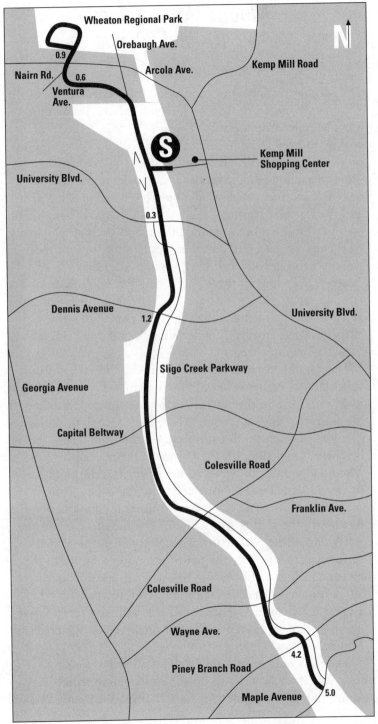

Sligo Creek Park

Wheaton Regional Park
Orebaugh Ave.
0.9
Arcola Ave.
Kemp Mill Road
Nairn Rd.   0.6
Ventura Ave.

S

Kemp Mill Shopping Center

University Blvd.

0.3

Dennis Avenue   1.2   University Blvd.

Sligo Creek Parkway

Georgia Avenue

Capital Beltway

Colesville Road

Franklin Ave.

Colesville Road

Wayne Ave.

Piney Branch Road   4.2

Maple Avenue   5.0

N

Mount Vernon Trail
15-, 16- and 20-mile tours

The Mount Vernon Trail runs along the western bank of the
Potomac River, from Roosevelt Island to George Washington's Mount Vernon estate. This trail is one of the most
heavily utilized trails in the area, and for good reason. Not
only is it scenic, with views of the major monuments and
other attractions, but it serves as a backbone connecting
busy work centers such as Washington, Rosslyn, Crystal City
and Alexandria. During weekday lunch hours, the trail is full
of office escapees out jogging, biking and skating. On sunny
weekends it seems like half the population is out on the
Mount Vernon Trail. It brings to mind Yogi Berra's old
quote: "No one goes there anymore—it's too crowded." For
family cycling, the crowds are generally not a problem, since
you will not be racing along the path. For more serious cyclists, dodging strollers, small children, and dogs will greatly
reduce your top speed.

The Mount Vernon Trail between Alexandria and Roosevelt Island is the most heavily used stretch. From Alexandria
to Mount Vernon the trail is much less crowded, although a
bit more challenging to ride. There are a few sharp hills, and
the home stretch south to Mount Vernon often brings brisk
headwinds whistling off the Potomac. Despite all this, the
Mount Vernon Trail is one of the premier cycling spots in
the area, loaded with family attractions. At the northern
end, Roosevelt Island has nature trails and hiking paths. Farther south the trail passes within a few hundred feet of the
north end of the main runway at National Airport; planes
seem to just skim over the path for landings. South of the
airport, Daingerfield Marina has sailboat and sailboard rentals, a restaurant and a playground. Old Town Alexandria is
a great lunch stop. Farther south you will pass Jones Point
lighthouse, Belle Haven Park, and finally reach the majestic
Mount Vernon estate.

The trail runs for a total of about 18 miles, making for a
long ride if you choose to do the entire round trip. I have
found that two 15-mile loops are the best for family cycling:

Roosevelt Island to Alexandria, and Belle Haven to Mount Vernon. Each of these paths have attractions every few miles, including food and rest rooms, allowing you to spend an entire day while making plenty of stops that will be fun for everyone. The northern section is best during the week; the trip to Mount Vernon is fun any time. Mount Vernon does draw a large number of tourists, so leave early or try to do this ride between September and May.

Roosevelt Island to Alexandria (15-mile tour)

Start:
Park your car at Roosevelt Island off the George Washington Parkway north, about a mile north of the Memorial Bridge.

Miles	Directions
0.0	From the Roosevelt Island parking lot, head south from the footbridge that crosses the Potomac River to the island. No bicycles are allowed on the island. There is a bike rack at the footbridge if you want to walk over to the island. It is worth the trip.
0.2	Bear left on the boardwalk surface.
0.5	Cross the channel on the small bridge. Great view of the Kennedy Center and the Lincoln Memorial.
0.9	Go under Memorial Bridge, trail narrows. This bridge was dedicated in 1932 to symbolize the union of the North and the South after the Civil War.
1.1	Stay straight on trail.
1.8	Navy-Marine Memorial on right.
1.9	Go over bridge. Trail narrows.
2.0	Stay straight on trail.

2.9   Pass Gravelly Point, with great view of National Airport. When the wind is to the north (as it usually is) jets will be landing almost on top of your helmet. There is often a snack truck in the parking lot. Continue through the parking lot, to the right of the white line, to rejoin trail.

3.5   Cross National Airport access road. There will be periodic road crossings for the next mile or so. Be careful: Airport traffic seems to always be in a hurry.

3.7   Stay straight on trail. The path to your left will take you to Crystal City.

4.8   Bear right on trail to go over bridge. The trail to the left (unmarked) will connect you to Four Mile Run Trail and the Washington and Old Dominion Trail.

5.7   Cross entrance to the Washington Sailing Marina at Daingerfield Island. There is a restaurant, rest rooms, picnic tables and sailboat rental here. On a warm (and windy) day you might want to rent a windsurfer.

5.9   Stay straight onto boardwalk surface.

6.1   Bear left on trail.

6.5   Pass by the PEPCO generating plant. Nice views across the Potomac.

6.9   Cross River Route. The trail switches to the right of the railroad tracks.

7.0   Cross street, trail continues straight ahead.

7.2	Turn left on Pendleton/Union Road at Oronoco Bay Park. The sidewalk is pretty poor, so on-road is your best bet. It is a short trip and the traffic is used to bicycle riders. Be sure to stop at all stop signs.
7.3	Cross Oronoco Street at Founders Park.
7.6	Stop at Torpedo Factory for arts and crafts. Lock bikes and walk to shops and visitor information center on King Street. To return, reverse directions, for a total ride of about 15 miles.

Belle Haven to Mount Vernon
(15-mile tour with 20-mile option)

This 15-mile round trip covers the southern, and most scenic, half of the Mount Vernon trail. The trail is less crowded but more hilly and not as well maintained as the more popular northern half. You can also make a short trip north from the starting point and visit Old Town Alexandria for lunch or shopping.

The start is at Belle Haven Park, which was a Scottish settlement that grew up around a tobacco warehouse in the 1730s. There are picnic areas, rest rooms and water fountains, a boat launching ramp, and bait for sale and boats for rent. Belle Haven is also adjacent to Dyke Marsh, a 240-acre bird-watchers paradise where over 250 species have been spotted. A hiking trail leads you through the marsh to the shores of the Potomac. The marsh is also home to beavers, muskrats, foxes and snapping turtles.

The midpoint of the ride is George Washington's Mount Vernon estate. This popular tourist destination is open every day of the year, even on Christmas. The admission is fairly steep, but the tour is worth the charge. Mount Vernon is a much more impressive sight from the river side, which you can't see unless you go inside the estate. I think there is some Southern protocol that calls the side of a house that faces the river the front of the house, regardless of which side of the house faces the road. Anyway, there is a snack bar, gift shop and the Mount Vernon Inn (a popular local restaurant) outside the estate if you don't choose to wander around the grounds. If one of your children is a Boy Scout, Mount Vernon has an approved historic trail for badge purposes.

Start:
Belle Haven Park parking lot. George Washington Memorial Parkway south of Alexandria. Turn left into park, make first left into parking lot. Park near rest rooms or anywhere along the path.

Miles	Directions
0.0	Head south (to the right) on the Mount Vernon paved trail from the parking lot.
0.1	Cross park entrance road. Trail gets a little bumpy for a while.
0.7	Ride on boardwalk through wetlands area. There will be several wooden bridges for some miles to come; wooden surfaces can be very slippery when wet.
1.0	Pass small parking area with telephone.
2.2	Path continues straight on low traffic road, beautiful houses on each side. Ride up slight hill. Note markers in road surface.
2.4	Turn right on Alexandria Avenue and cross bridge over the parkway. Turn left to get back on paved path immediately over bridge. For the next few miles, the path will cross parkway access roads. Be very careful—traffic to and from the parkway moves quickly.
2.8	River Farms Garden Park is to your left, across the parkway.

4.0 Nice view of the Potomac River as the trail turns away from the river for a short stretch.

4.5 Curvy downhill run to a bridge, followed by a short, steep uphill grind.

4.8 Cross road at Fort Hunt. This 156-acre park has many picnic areas and hiking trails.

4.9 Ride on park road to go under bridge and immediately get back on path to the left past bridge.

5.0 Ride on boardwalk path paralleling river. Nice view of wide stretch of the Potomac River.

6.1 Restaurant to the right across the parkway.

6.6 Parking area with picnic benches, portable rest room and exercise course. Unless you are desperate, hold on—only one more mile to Mount Vernon.

7.5 Steep uphill climb guards the entrance to Mount Vernon, but it is a pleasant ride through cedar and pine trees.

7.6 Brick wall announces entrance to Mount Vernon.

7.7 Reach parking lot. Ride carefully through parking lot; at the far end there are bike racks. It is a short walk to Mount Vernon, with several historic markers along the way. Follow the path in the reverse direction to get back to your car for a 15-mile tour.

15.4 If you want to visit Alexandria, continue north on trail past Belle Haven.

16.2	Cross bridge. The path winds along an apartment complex.
16.3	Path is on the sidewalk for a bit. Turn right at South Street. For the next one and a half miles you will be riding on roads with traffic.
16.7	Turn left onto South Royal Street. Follow road under Beltway bridge. If you are a serious lighthouse fanatic, turn right immediately after going under bridge and follow the road to the Jones Point Lighthouse. This is not a very dramatic lighthouse, being more house than light. This was once the southernmost point of the old District of Columbia. Nice views of the river, but all in all not a must-see spot.
16.8	Continue on South Royal, cross Green Street.
16.9	Cross Jefferson Street.
17.0	Cross Franklin Street.
17.1	Cross Gibbon Street.
17.2	Turn right onto Wilkes Street, go through neat-looking tunnel with several historic markers. Caution: It is dark in this short tunnel.
17.3	Reach South Union Street; turn left. Playground is on right.
17.5	Bike shop to the right at Duke Street.
17.7	Reach King Street and downtown Alexandria. Retrace directions back to Belle Haven Park for a 20-mile total ride.

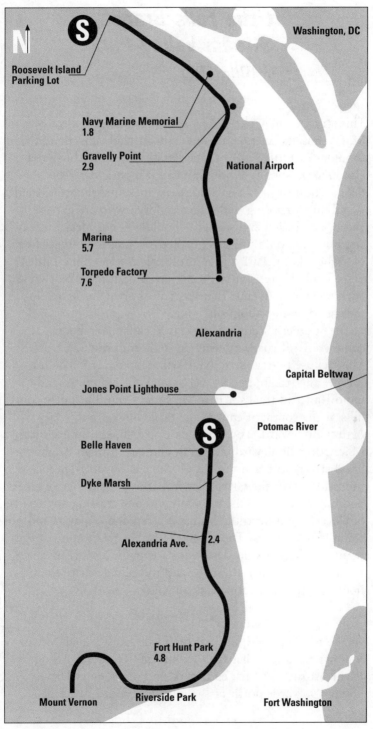

Mount Vernon Trail

N

Washington, DC

Roosevelt Island
Parking Lot

Navy Marine Memorial
1.8

Gravelly Point
2.9

National Airport

Marina
5.7

Torpedo Factory
7.6

Alexandria

Capital Beltway

Jones Point Lighthouse

Potomac River

Belle Haven

Dyke Marsh

Alexandria Ave.   2.4

Fort Hunt Park
4.8

Mount Vernon   **Riverside Park**   **Fort Washington**

Little Falls Branch Stream Valley Park
7-mile tour

This stream valley park has a split personality. North of Massachusetts Avenue, the hiker/biker trail runs along the shoulder of Little Falls Branch Parkway, a fairly busy road, although personally I wouldn't call it a parkway. This 1.5-mile section from Massachusetts Avenue to Arlington Road is suitable for riding with older children who are experienced, controlled cyclists. The shoulder is not ideal for trailers, but you could use this northern section to connect from Norwood Local Park to the southern section of the Little Falls Trail. There is an off-road paved path from Norwood Park to Dorset Avenue that lets you shorten the shoulder mileage down to about one mile.

The southern section of the Little Falls hiker/biker path is completely off-road, a scenic 1.2-mile trail running from Massachusetts Avenue to MacArthur Boulevard. The trail follows the stream bed as well as the old Baltimore and Ohio Railroad tracks. There are some steep (but fairly short) hills at the southern end, as the trail climbs up to Mac-Arthur Boulevard. You can then ride a short distance on the MacArthur Boulevard bike path and cut through neighborhood streets to reach the C&O Canal Towpath. There is a footbridge over the Clara Barton Parkway that allows hikers and bikers to get to the towpath without crossing any roads; however, the trail to the bridge is steep and unpaved and not suitable for trailers. The footbridge takes you to one of the many lockkeeper's houses on the towpath, a short distance from the rapids at Little Falls and the island where the Canoe Cruisers Association has a facility.

Start:
At the northern end, park at the Little Falls Branch Stream Valley parking lot, between Hillandale Road and Arlington Road. At the southern end, park on Fort Sumner Drive, about 100 yards north of the intersection of Little Falls

Branch Parkway and Massachusetts Avenue. Ride south on the sidewalk to connect to the trail.

Miles	Directions
0.0	From Little Falls Branch Stream Valley Park parking lot, cross Little Falls Branch Parkway to hiker/biker path on shoulder.
0.5	Cross Dorset Avenue.
0.9	Cross River Road, continue on shoulder.
1.4	Cross Massachusetts Avenue. Path is directly across street. Parking for southern section is via path to your right, under bridge.
2.1	Bear right on path and cross bridge.
2.4	Go under railroad bridge. Steep hills begin here.
2.6	Reach MacArthur Boulevard. Cross at traffic light to MacArthur Boulevard bike path on south side of road.
2.8	Turn left onto Maryland Avenue. This low-traffic neighborhood street curves to the left and becomes Ridge Drive.
3.5	Pass 61st Street on Ridge Drive and look for path opening through guard rail on your right. Walk bikes down this steep, dirt path to the footbridge across the Clara Barton Parkway. The path leads directly to the C&O Canal Towpath.

Little Falls Branch Stream Valley Park

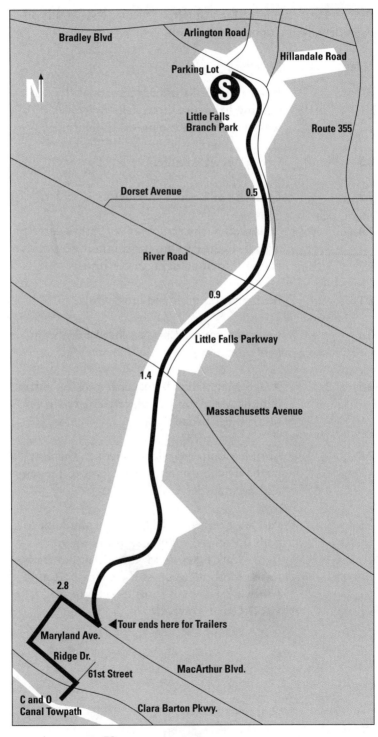

Adelphi Mill
4-mile tours

This is actually part of the Northwest Branch Stream Valley Park, with Adelphi Mill at the middle of the hiker/biker trail. Located on Riggs Road, the Adelphi Mill was built in 1796 and operated through at least 1811. This attractive stone building has been restored and maintained and is now used as a community center and meeting place. Heading north (to the right) on the path from the parking lot takes you along a fitness trail and past a rest stop and several playgrounds. In this direction the trail ends abruptly just short of the Washington Beltway, with a steep gravel path going uphill into a local neighborhood.

If you turn left on the path from the Adelphi Mill parking lot and head south, the trail will follow and then cross the Northwest Branch of the Anacostia River and then take you through several interesting parks. The first is the Adelphi Manor Community Recreation Center, with a small playground and a large field where cricket games are often held. After you cross University Boulevard, you will come to the Lane Manor Community Recreation Center, which has a pool, tennis courts, baseball fields and several playgrounds. Lane Manor also has paths that cross over into the University Hills Neighborhood Park, with a duck pond and several modern playgrounds.

Start:
Adelphi Mill Historic Site, Adelphi, Md. Take Route 193, University Boulevard, south from the Washington Beltway, I-495. Cross Route 650, New Hampshire Avenue, and then turn left onto Riggs Road. The parking area will be on your left after going down the hill.

North Along the Fitness Trail

Miles	Directions
0.0	Turn right from the parking lot on the path along the stream.

0.3	There is a playground over the bridge on the right.
0.6	You can splash through the water here or take the bridge over. Guess which route your kids will probably take.
0.8	Go under New Hampshire Avenue and then Carroll Avenue.
2.0	The trail ends abruptly here. You can lock your bikes to a tree and follow the foot path along the river, or turn around and go back. The path leading up the hill ends in a local neighborhood.

South to Lane Manor Park

Miles	Directions
0.0	Turn left from the parking lot on the path along the stream and immediately go under Riggs Road.
0.5	Go over the bridge into Adelphi Manor Park, playground on right.
0.7	Cross University Boulevard. Caution: heavy traffic. There is a pool to the left and several playgrounds. Take one of the paths to the left to cut over to University Hills Park and feed the ducks or go to a large, modern playground.
1.3	The trail splashes through a few small trickles that will be wet and muddy after rain of any significance.
2.0	Go under East West Highway.
2.1	The trail ends at Ager Road and a parking lot with a small playground.

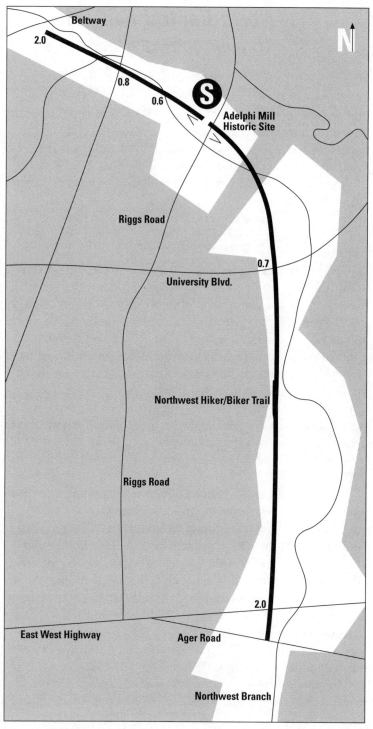

Beltway

2.0

0.8

0.6

S

Adelphi Mill
Historic Site

Riggs Road

0.7

University Blvd.

Northwest Hiker/Biker Trail

Riggs Road

2.0

East West Highway

Ager Road

Northwest Branch

N

North Central Rail Trail
16-mile one-way ride

If I had to pick one ride to recommend in this entire book, this would be it. The North Central Rail Trail combines convenience, history and lush scenery to make this a dynamite family ride. We have never grown tired of riding on this trail, and on each ride we discover something new. Part of Gunpowder Falls State Park, the trail has become such an attraction that it seems to have spurred a lot of creative thinking by the park rangers. On almost every weekend, guided hikes are available, and there are often craft shows and special events.

Opened only six years after the Baltimore and Ohio Railroad (the first commercial railroad in the U.S.), the North Central Railroad connected Baltimore with York and Gettysburg, Pennsylvania. The rail line ran for 134 years, playing a major role in the Civil War. The NCRR carried Abraham Lincoln to Gettysburg to deliver his famous speech and carried his body back to Illinois via Gettysburg after his assassination. The railroad followed the path of three small rivers (Beetree Run, Little Falls and Gunpowder Falls), using many small bridges to span these narrow waterways. In 1972 Hurricane Agnes caused tremendous flooding, and the cost of repairing the damaged bridges was the death knell for the NCRR.

The railroad's loss has been turned into cycling's gain, for the many rebuilt bridges provide extensive views of the rivers and valleys. The rail station at Monkton has been renovated and turned into a visitor's center, and many historic buildings can be seen at the old railroad towns along the trails. The trail runs for slightly more than 20 miles, ending abruptly at the Mason-Dixon line at the Pennsylvania border. Not far from the trail is Boordy Vineyards, located in Hyde. Boordy has hour-long tours of the 16-acre vineyard, with free wine tastings. Maryland's largest and oldest winery is open Monday through Saturday, from 10 A.M. to 5 P.M.

The only downside to this trail is that parking can be tricky. There is parking at Ashland, Papermill Road, Phoe-

nix, Sparks, Glencoe, Monkton, White Hall, Parkton, Bentley Springs and Freeland (described from north to south).
The Ashland and Monkton lots are the most popular, and
they fill up early in the morning in the summer. Our favorite
way to do this trail is to combine with another family and
use two or more cars. We leave one car at the Ashland lot
and then jam everyone into the other car(s) and go up to the
Bentley Springs lot. We then cycle the 15 miles or so down
to Ashland and send a few of the adults back via car to re-
trieve the other automobiles. The trail route described below
is for just that trip, but you can easily create your own using
the directions to each parking spot provided below.

Start:

Bentley Springs, Md. Take York Road, Route 45, north from
Shawan Road. Turn left (west) onto Bentley Road or Kaufman Road. Follow Bentley or Kaufman to Five Corners,
then follow Bentley Road to the parking lot. To get to
Monkton at the southern end, take York Road north from
Shawan Road. Take Monkton Road east for three miles to
the trail crossing and parking lot. This lot fills quickly, but
there you can ask for directions to other parking areas. Gunpowder Falls State Park telephone is 410-592-2897 (TDD:
410-974-3683).

Miles	Directions
0.0	Start at the Bentley Springs parking area. Turn left (south) on trail.
0.2	Cross Bentley Road.
1.4	Cross Walker Road.
2.4	After going under I-83 bridge, pass through exercise course. Cross Dairy Road, next to Owl Branch bridge.
2.8	Pass through Parkton and trail access parking lot. Nice views of Little Falls south of here. Steep terrain on both sides of the trail.

3.6	Small waterfall and pool on the right. A picnic table and a trail to the river's edge make this a nice rest stop.
4.5	Cross Weisburg Road. If it feels like you are pedalling harder, you are; the trail has changed from a slight downhill grade to nearly flat.
4.9	Pass through White Hall and trail access parking lot. The river takes a jog to the west here, out of sight, but the view to the east makes up for it.
5.2	Cross Hunter Mill Road.
6.0	Cross Hicks Road.
6.5	Cross Blue Mount Road. Little Falls leaves the trail, replaced by Gunpowder Falls.
8.5	Enter Monkton. The renovated rail station is on your right, serving as a ranger and visitor's center. Inside you can see exhibits on the history of North Central Railroad, buy T-shirts, maps and souvenirs, or fill your water bottles from the pump. Across the parking lot is a combination antique and snack shop, as well as Monkton Bike Rentals. There you can get your bike repaired, buy a bell or rent a tandem.
9.3	Pass through Corbett. This small town is listed on the National Register of Historic Places, as is Monkton.
11.2	Pass through Glencoe, an old resort area featuring houses from the 1870s.

12.0	Pass through Sparks and trail access parking lot. The historic Sparks bank is across the street, owned by the park and soon to be renovated. South of Sparks, Carroll Creek runs into Gunpowder Falls, making this a popular fishing area.
13.8	Pass through Phoenix and trail access parking lot.
14.9	Ruins of an old lime kiln on right.
15.4	Cross Paper Mill Road. Some parking along the road.
15.8	Reach the end of the trail at Ashland.

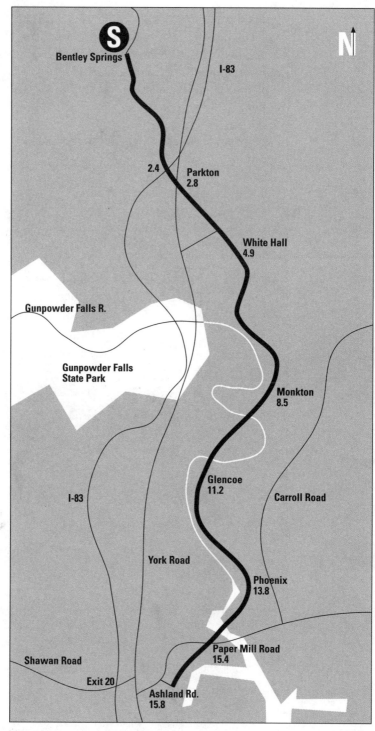

S
Bentley Springs

N

I-83

2.4 Parkton
     2.8

White Hall
4.9

Gunpowder Falls R.

Gunpowder Falls
State Park

Monkton
8.5

Glencoe
11.2

Carroll Road

I-83

York Road

Phoenix
13.8

Paper Mill Road
15.4

Shawan Road

Exit 20

Ashland Rd.
15.8

Druid Hill Park
4-mile loop

Located on one of the highest spots in Baltimore, this faded beauty of a park is well past its prime. Druid Hill Park has gone through many boom-to-bust cycles in its 132 years of existence, and it seems to be undergoing a resurgence recently. Home to the Baltimore Zoo and Conservatory, Druid Hill has had a checkered past over the years. Established in 1860, this 650-acre park is one of the three largest urban green spaces in the U.S. The park is covered with mature, majestic oak trees, which are at the root of the park's name, since oaks were sacred to the Druids!

The Baltimore Zoo is the third oldest in the U.S., after the Philadelphia and Cincinnati zoos. It is a large zoo, with all the usual zoo stuff. Before they were turned into a zoo, the grounds were part of the park, and in the zoo you will see many ornate pavilions and other buildings that were once boat houses and train stations. Just outside the zoo is a conservatory featuring an exotic orchid garden and many other colorful plants in its extensive greenhouses. The fruit area is amazing; in the middle of January, you can see lemons the size of grapefruits.

Druid Hill Park itself has over 30 miles of low-traffic park roads for pleasant bicycle riding, although they are fairly hilly. There are several playgrounds and recreation areas and a road around Druid Hill Lake that is closed to cars. The park attracts an urban crowd, and parking is tight on weekends when many people wax their cars, walk their dogs and play with their kids. A ride around the park is an architectural buff's delight, with many ornate pavilions and funky statues.

Start:
Druid Hill Park, Baltimore, Md. Take Martin Luther King Boulevard north from downtown Baltimore. Turn right onto McCulloh Street, Route 129. Turn right on Cloverdale and left into park entrance. The lake and parking area are to the right of the flagpole inside the park. Baltimore Zoo telephone is 410-366-LION.

Miles	Directions
0.0	Start at the parking area next to the lake.
0.2	Great view across Baltimore. The structure on your left is Baltimore Tower.
0.5	Short stretch on roadway. Stay to the right; you may have to go around parked cars.
0.7	Return to park path.
1.0	Go straight past the flagpole and head uphill. Bear right at the one-way sign.
1.6	Go past zoo administration building and zoo areas on your right.
2.1	Turn right at the stop sign.
2.3	On the right are some barriers to an old road. Go around the barriers and ride on the road behind the conservatory.
2.6	The road ends and the path curves left. To the right, a path takes you to the road that leads to the zoo entrance.
2.8	Arrive at main zoo entrance and parking lots. Lock bikes and visit the zoo. When you leave, retrace your path on the park road, but go straight when you come to the point where you left the path.
3.1	Conservatory on your left, well worth a visit.
3.4	Turn left at stop sign.
3.6	Go around barriers to enter lake loop path.
4.0	Return to parking area.

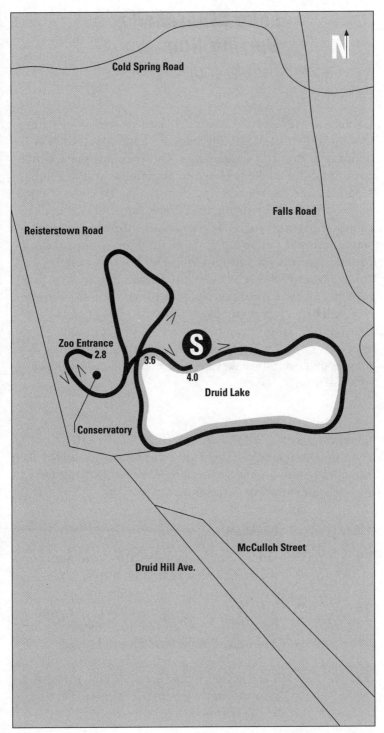

N

Cold Spring Road

Falls Road

Reisterstown Road

Zoo Entrance
2.8

3.6

S

4.0

Druid Lake

Conservatory

McCulloh Street

Druid Hill Ave.

Lake Montebello/ Herring Run
6-mile loop

Located in the beautiful Mayfield Gardens section of Baltimore, just east of Memorial Stadium, Lake Montebello is a popular cycling and skating area. On weekends the 1.3-mile road around the lake is closed to automobile traffic and has separate lanes for runners and cyclists. The lake was formed in the late 1800s by damming Tiffany Run and was used to supply water to the city. The remains of the old pumping station are still visible along the road. Water from Lake Montebello was used to fill Druid Hill Lake as well.

Lake Montebello is adjacent to Herring Run Park, a 550-acre greenway that was turned into parkland in the early 1890s. The bicycle path along Herring Run was one of the first built in Baltimore, and in places it shows its age. However, this stream valley path does take you to a number of playgrounds, and it makes for a nice loop along both sides of the stream.

Start:
Lake Montebello, Baltimore, Md. Take Charles Street north from downtown Baltimore. Turn right onto 33rd Street. Pass Memorial Stadium and go straight at Hillen Road to Lake Montebello entrance. Park on perimeter road.

Miles	Directions
0.0	Enter Lake Montebello from 33rd Street and park on the left side of loop road.
0.8	Turn left at the stop sign onto Lake Montebello Drive. Get on the sidewalk on the left, and immediately turn left at Harford Road.
1.2	Turn left onto the first path that goes down into the Herring Run parking lot. Turn left at the bottom.

1.3	Go under Harford Road on the small bridge under the center arch.
1.4	Bear left on the path.
2.1	Stay straight on path.
2.2	Cross Belair Road.
2.6	Cross Mannasota Avenue.
2.7	Cross Brehm's Lane. Small playground on left.
2.9	Another small playground on left.
3.1	Arrive at Sinclair Lane. The trail continues for another half mile, where it dead ends in a rather unattractive industrial area. Turn around here and follow the path back to Belair Road.
4.0	Cross Belair Road and turn right on the sidewalk and go over Herring Run on the sidewalk. Turn left onto the path immediately after you cross over the river.
4.9	Go under the Harford Road bridge and turn left. Go over the same small bridge from mile 1.3.
5.0	Turn right on path immediately after you cross the bridge.
5.2	Cross Harford Road at the traffic light. Directly to your right is Lake Montebello Drive. Turn left to reenter Lake Montebello.
5.3	Turn left onto loop road.
5.8	Return to start.

Lake Montebello/Herring Run

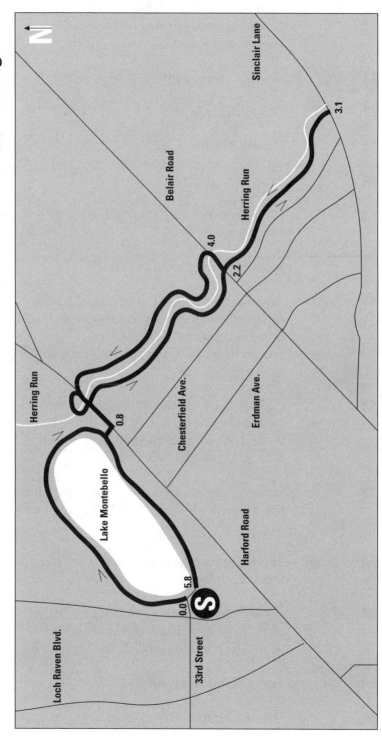

Patapsco State Park
4-mile loop

The Patapsco River played a key role in the development of
Baltimore as a major harbor and also pops up in many other
bits of history, earning it the title River of History. The river
provided transportation and food for Piscataway, Susque-
hannock and Seneca Indians and was first explored by Cap-
tain John Smith in 1608. The river was originally called
Bolus Flu, after the jagged red clay cliffs of what is now
known as Federal Hill, along Baltimore's Inner Harbor.
Somewhere along the way the river regained its Indian name,
Patapsco, a good thing for the many people of the Patapsco
Valley. I doubt that property values would be as high if the
area was known as the Bolus Flu Valley.

The Patapsco River begins at Parr's Spring, near Mt. Airy,
runs past Fort McHenry, where Francis Scott Key was in-
spired to write the "Star Spangled Banner," and empties into
the Chesapeake Bay at Sparrow's Point. The Patapsco Valley
State Park system covers over 11,000 acres, with a number
of recreational areas along the river's path, all of which are
great spots to spend the day, and several of which are popular destinations for cyclists. The McKeldin area, located on
Marriotsville Road north of I-70, has a five-mile signed hiking trail that is a popular ride for mountain bikers. The Hol-
lofield area also has several trails that are very hilly, but
open to cyclists.

The Avalon area is the best bet for family cycling. This
section of the park features a road that runs along the Patapsco and is closed to vehicle traffic. Actually, Hurricane
Agnes closed this road for good at Bloede's dam in 1972,
and it is now a great spot for leisurely cycling. There is a
swinging bridge across the river that leads to a paved hiker/
biker trail and a popular, and rugged, mountain biking trail
along the river. The rail line along the park is still active and
you will often see mile-long strings of freight cars being
pulled along by multiple locomotives. There are fishing
areas, playgrounds and picnic shelters, as well. Entering the
park, you will pass under the Thomas Viaduct, built in 1835

and now designated as a National Historic Landmark. This bridge over the Patapsco stretches over 600 feet and was the biggest railroad bridge in the world when it was opened. Legend has it that hundreds of spectators came to the official opening, convinced that the bridge would collapse when a steam locomotive chugged across it. The bridge withstood the six-ton load, and now over a sesquicentury later regularly carries 300-ton diesel locomotives.

Start:

Take the Route I-66 east exit (exit 47) from I-95 south of Baltimore and head east. Exit onto Route 1 south (exit 3) and turn right at South Street. Immediately turn left into the park entrance. Patapsco Valley State Park telephone is 410-461-5005.

Miles	Directions
0.0	Start at the parking lot near shelter 105 and the rest rooms. Turn right onto the road and ride around the gates.
1.6	Reach swinging bridge on right. The path continues ahead for .9 miles and dead-ends at the Bloede dam, which is currently being rebuilt. Turn right and walk bikes over the swinging bridge.
1.7	At the northern end of the bridge, the foot path to the left is a popular mountain biking path that follows the river for miles. Unless this is a mountain bike trip for you, turn right onto the asphalt path.
2.4	Go over a small bridge, with a spooky little tunnel to your left.
3.1	Lost Lake fishing area.
3.6	Turn right at stop sign.

3.7   Turn right into parking lot. The small road to the left dead-ends less than one-half mile east at Lawyers Hill Road.

3.8   Return to start.

Patapsco State Park

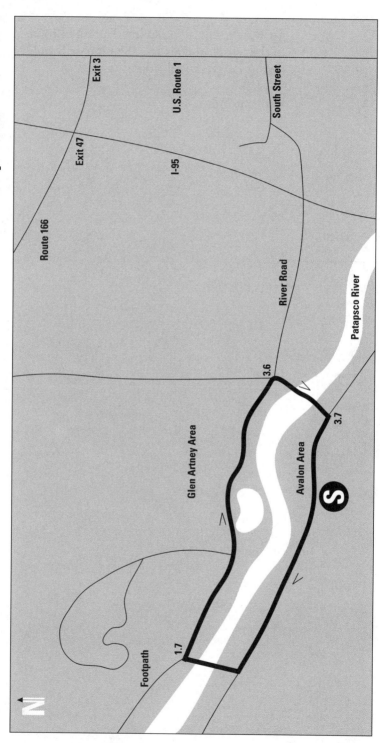

Magruder Branch Stream Valley Park
6-mile tour

If you have ever wondered why you don't see many squirrels in this area, it is because they are all in the Magruder Branch Stream Valley. This attractive three-mile-long asphalt path starts in Damascus Recreational Park, and within half a mile dives down to amble along the Magruder Stream Valley. To preserve the wetlands along the stream, much of the path is actually on boardwalks, which are fun to ride on but require a little extra care when stroller pushers and dog walkers are on the path.

The starting point, Damascus Recreational Park, has several nice playgrounds and ball fields, but no water fountains; bring drinks. There are no playgrounds along the path; in fact, there is only one bench along the three-mile stretch! Think of this route as a nature trail you can do on bicycles. In the fall, the colors are phenomenal, and in the early mornings you can often see deer drinking from the stream.

If you are riding with older children or experienced cyclists, Route 27 is a pretty nice road to cycle on. There is a lot of high-speed traffic, but the shoulder is wide and smooth. From Sweepstakes Road you can connect to Route 27. It is then a three-mile ride over rolling hills to downtown Damascus, a pretty little town with many fine places to eat. I do not recommend this ride for inexperienced cyclists or young children. When you are in the Damascus/Mount Airy area, stop in at Mount Airy Bicycles. Larry Black, the owner, and his wife Linda give seminars on family cycling and can often be seen on their bicycle built for four pulling a trailer behind them. Larry's shop has the widest selection of trailers, kiddie seats and tandems in this area.

Start:
Damascus Regional Park, Damascus, Md. Take Ridge Road, Route 27, north from Frederick Road, Route 355. Turn right at Kings Valley Road and turn left into first park en-

trance. Park in either parking lot. Telephone is 301-972-6581.

Miles	Directions
0.0	Get on asphalt path next to gravel road that leaves parking lot at rear. Playground to the right.
0.4	Cross gravel road at top of hill. Long downhill stretch ahead.
1.0	Go over bridge; path takes a sharp left.
1.6	Cross Sweepstakes Road, trail continues to the right.
2.6	View the only bench on this trail!
3.0	Valley Park Road. A short piece of trail goes to a picnic table .2 miles ahead; not worth the ride. Retrace trail to return to start.

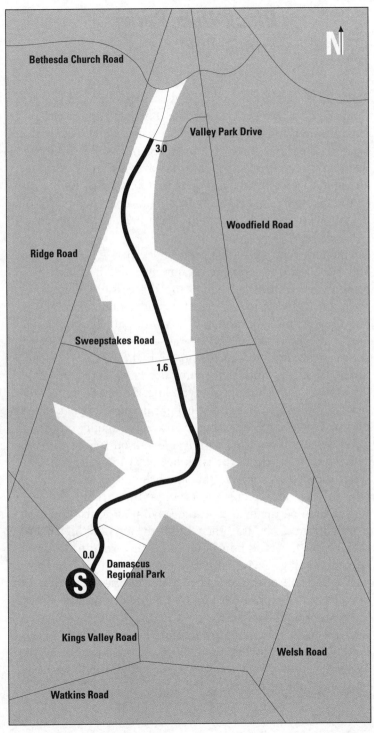

Bethesda Church Road

N

Valley Park Drive

3.0

Woodfield Road

Ridge Road

Sweepstakes Road

1.6

0.0 Damascus
Regional Park

S

Kings Valley Road

Welsh Road

Watkins Road

Black Hills Park
7-mile loop

Black Hills Park is one of the newest parks in Montgomery County and a real gem. Located in Boyds, the park is centered around 505-acre Little Seneca Lake, which was built as both a recreational lake and an emergency water supply for the metropolitan area. The lake has over 15 miles of shoreline and a water capacity of 4.25 billion gallons. As big as it is, the lake only covers less than one-third of the area of this heavily wooded park. It is well worth the visit, with or without bicycles.

The park rents rowboats and canoes on a seasonal basis, and there is a boat launching ramp available if you wish to bring your own boat. A handicapped-accessible pontoon boat, *The Osprey*, is available for tours of the lake. Boat rental, launching and pontoon boat rides all charge nominal fees. The lake is stocked with bass, catfish and bluegill; fishing maps are available at the boat rental facility.

The park is as hilly as its name promises, and it makes for a lot of gear shifting when cycling. The park roads are smooth and wide, and traffic is light if you choose to ride on the road. The route described below stays mainly on the paved hiker/biker trails, both inside and outside of the park. The paved trail within the park begins at the park office and skirts the eastern shore of the lake behind the visitor center. Stop in the visitor center for a look at the exhibits and the turtles sunning themselves in the small pond outside the front entrance. The trail then winds through the hills overlooking the lake and puts you on the park road for a short stretch, passing several large playgrounds and picnic areas.

The last half of the tour goes over a short, steep stretch of gravelly path before returning to a paved path that follows the eastern boundary of the park. There you can connect with the Waters Landing community bike path that circles Lake Churchill, passing a few more playgrounds on the way. You are very likely to see deer, geese and groundhogs at almost any time of day along this route.

Start:

The park is located off of Old Baltimore Road in northern Montgomery County. From I-270 north, take the Route 118 east exit and turn left at Route 355, Frederick Road. Bear left at the junction with Route 27 and in about a mile turn left onto Old Baltimore Road. The park entrance is on the left a few hundred yards after you pass under I-270. Park in the parking lot next to the first playground you see on your left at the intersection of the Lake Ridge Drive loop, about one mile from the park entrance. Black Hills Park telephone is 301-972-9396.

Miles	Directions
0.0	From the playground parking lot turn right on Lake Ridge Drive, heading back towards the park entrance. In about 100 yards at the top of the hill you will see the park office on your left and the beginning of the hiker/biker trail. Turn left into the park office parking lot and turn left onto the trail. An exhilarating downhill stretch awaits you.
0.2	Turn left at the bottom of the hill. The path to the right dead-ends at the lake shore.
0.5	The visitor center is on your left, and the boat docks are on your right. Where the trail reaches a T, turn left and then right to continue on the main trail.
0.6	Bear right around the rest rooms; the trail enters the woods.
0.9	Turn right on the trail before your reach Picnic Lane, and ride through one of those ubiquitous exercise courses. Great views of the lake through the trees.
1.2	The trail ends at Picnic Drive; turn right and follow the road.

1.3   Turn right onto Lake Ridge Drive. The next .7 of a mile will be on the park road.

1.4   The road bobs up and down. Large playgrounds and picnic areas are on the left.

1.7   Climb a pretty steep hill and reach Lake Ridge Drive where you started. Turn right and head towards the entrance again, this time continuing past the park office and down the hill.

2.0   Black Hill Road is on your left; on your right a path goes into the woods. Take the path into the woods. The first few hundred feet is level and smooth, but it quickly turns into a steep gravel path. Walk your bike; I don't recommend this section for trailers.

2.2   Ride on a wooden bridge over the stream, leading to a short, rocky uphill section before you return to a paved bike path.

2.3   At the top of the hill, turn right on the blessedly smooth, level path. For the next mile or so, suburbia reigns supreme, with town houses and quarter-acre lots on your left. On your right, turtles will be sunning themselves on rocks and ducks will be paddling through the rushes. Cross your fingers—this section is new, but man and nature are coexisting nicely here.

3.4   Turn right over a wooden bridge.

3.7   Small tot lot on left, where path curves.

3.8   Cross Wynnfield Drive and leave Black Hills Park. Across the street, the Waters Landing community bike path begins along Lake Churchill.

4.2	Bear right on the path and cross over a wooden bridge. A steep hill follows.
4.3	Continue straight on path. A playground and community pool is on your left.
4.4	Turn right on the path at the road.
4.5	Turn right on the path before you reach the townhouses. The path narrows in this section as it passes behind the townhouse development. Ride carefully, there are usually small domestic animals roaming about.
4.9	Turn right over the wooden bridge.
5.1	Bear right on the path where Lake Churchill ends. On the other side of the lake, the trail passes over a very rough culvert. Immediately after the culvert make a very sharp left turn to return to Wynnfield Drive. Cross the street and return to the Black Hills hiker/biker path.
5.5	Cross wooden bridge and bear left on trail.
6.6	Return to woods on steep rocky path down to the bridge over the stream. Walk your bikes down this section.
6.7	Cross bridge. Begin steep uphill on gravel surface. Walk your bikes.
6.9	Turn left on Lake Ridge Drive and begin short uphill climb.
7.2	Return to playground parking lot.

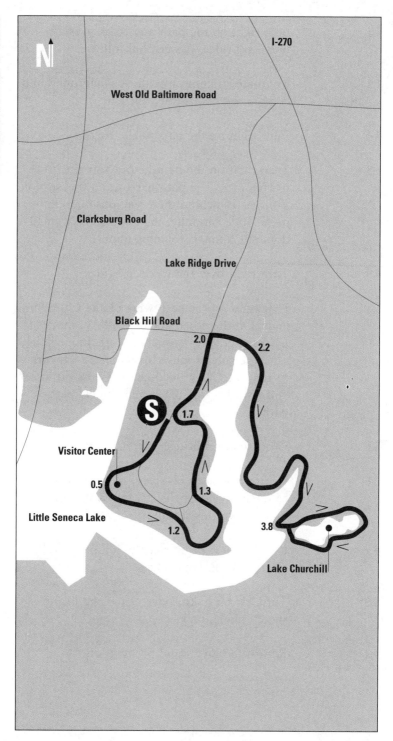

Black Hills Park

N

I-270

West Old Baltimore Road

Clarksburg Road

Lake Ridge Drive

Black Hill Road

2.0
2.2

S
1.7

Visitor Center

0.5

1.3

Little Seneca Lake

1.2

3.8

Lake Churchill

Seneca Creek State Park
5-mile loop

The history of the Seneca Valley typifies that of much of Upper Montgomery County. Swift running streams and fertile valley lands supported thriving Indian communities for thousands of years. European settlers began moving in during the late 1600s and used the fields to grow tobacco, fruit and grains and harnessed the streams to power grist mills. Seneca Creek powered several mills, and you can still see the remains of the Clopper Grist Mill and Black Rock Mill along the creek.

Seneca Creek State Park has been developed along 12 miles of the creek, with a dam that forms the 90-acre Clopper Lake. The park rents boats for fishing and recreation during the summer and runs pontoon boat tours as well. There are several picnic areas and playgrounds, miles of hiking and mountain bike paths, and a 30-acre, 18-hole disc golf course. The visitor center has interpretative programs and self-guided nature and history hikes.

This is a beautiful park, another one that is worth a visit with or without a bicycle. There are no separate bicycle paths; the tour described below follows the low-traffic park roads, which, barring holidays, are perfect for cycling with children. There are a few hills but nothing terribly strenuous. You can also ride bicycles on the hiking trails in the park. Two are particularly nice for families: Lake Shore Trail (.75 miles) and the Mink Hollow Trail (1.25 miles). These are fairly easy trails for novice mountain bike riders, but I don't recommend doing any mountain biking with a child in a child carrier. Pulling a trailer is definitely out of the question. These paths are perfect for preteens and teenagers.

Start:
From I-270 take the Clopper Road West exit. The park entrance is located on Clopper Road between Longdraft Road and Great Seneca Highway. There is parking immediately inside the entrance, before the ranger contact station. If this area is full, park at the boat center parking area (you will

have to pay the entrance fee). For Seneca Creek information,
call 301-924-2127 (TDD: 301-974-3683).

Miles	Directions
0.0	Park entrance. If you park outside the entrance station you will save the admission fee. There are not many spots here, however. If it is full, begin at the parking lot at the .5 mile spot.
0.3	Turn right on park road.
0.5	Parking lot on left, with playground, boat rentals and an inviting pine grove with picnic tables, grills and paths down to the lake.
0.9	Kingfisher overlook with great photo opportunities on left. On your left, directly opposite the sign for the Nuthatch and Bluejay areas, you will see the starting points for the Mink Hollow and Lake Shore trails. The Lake Shore Trail runs back to the boat rental area, through farm fields and a few hills. The Mink Hollow Trail is a little more challenging, going through fields, forest and a marsh before reaching a picnic area.
1.7	Turn right at stop sign.
1.9	Parking lot for disc golf. Bring a frisbee along and try it out. It is like a combination of basketball and golf.
2.1	Return to park road and go straight where the exit sign points to the left. This will take you on a loop through several playgrounds and heavily wooded picnic areas.

3.2   Turn right as the loop ends.

3.6   Turn right at the stop sign.

5.3   Return to park entrance.

Seneca Creek State Park

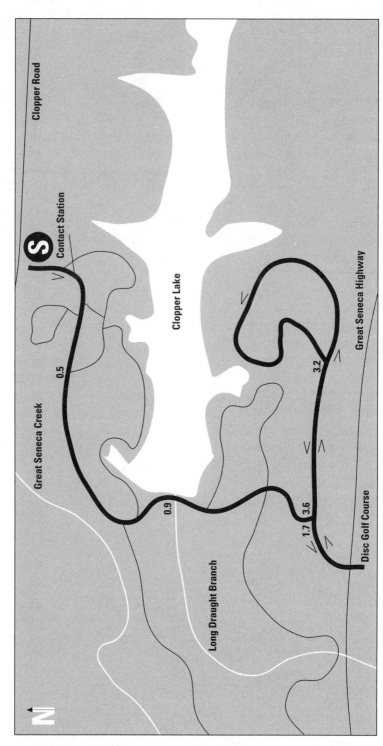

Indian Creek/
Lake Artemesia
6-mile tour

Located in the heart of northern Prince Georges County, this
combination of a stream valley park and a renovated hole in
the ground is a scenic oasis just a stone's throw from busy
Route 1. The paved section of the path stretches from Riverdale Road to Greenbelt Road, passing many neighborhood
playgrounds and recreation centers, as well as curving
around the runways of College Park Airport, the oldest airport in the country.

Heading south from Greenbelt Road, the trail follows Indian Creek for about a mile and then crosses the creek at the
entrance to Lake Artemesia Park. This park is one of the
real gems in the Washington area. More commonly known
as Lake Metro, this 38-acre lake was created as a result of
construction for the Metro subway system Green Line, which
will run through College Park to Greenbelt. When Metro
needed sand and gravel to construct the track bed and parking lots for the new stations, it was determined that the soil
in the Paint Branch and Indian Creek Stream Valley Park
was of the right type for the construction. In a cooperative
agreement that was actually cheaper than trucking in mate-
rials, Metro agreed to convert the land into a park after the
excavation was completed.

The name Lake Artemesia comes from Mrs. Artemesia
Newman, the wife of Edmond Newman, who stocked the
original lake with bass and goldfish. Today an enlarged Lake
Artemesia is the centerpiece of a beautiful park, with hiking
and biking paths, rest rooms and a concession area, a model
boat basin, and lovely landscaping. To get to the park you
have to walk or ride a bicycle; the closest parking lot is a
fifth of a mile away at Berwyn Road.

Start:
Riverdale Recreation Center. Take Riverdale Road west
from the Baltimore Washington Parkway (I-295) north of
the Washington Beltway. Turn right after 1.5 miles onto 51st

Street. Turn into the Recreation Center and park in the lot at the left rear of the park. For park information, call Department of Parks and Recreation at 301-699-2407. For Lake Artemesia information, call 301-345-6985 (TDD: 301-445-4512).

Miles	Directions
0.0	From the parking lot, head north on the trail that exits at the northeast corner of the parking lot.
0.2	Go under bridge.
0.7	Pass through a fitness course; the Dennis Wolf rest stop is on your right. On your left is the parking lot for the Linson pool and the Wells ice rink.
0.9	Go under Calvert Road. Bear right when the path forks.
1.2	The trail loops around the runway of the College Park Airport. The interesting-looking building to the left is the 94th Aero Squadron restaurant.
1.5	Go straight over bridge.
1.7	Turn left into Lake Artemesia Park. Go straight on path.
2.0	Model boat basin, concession area, rest rooms, lake walk. Trails circle the lake and there are several places to sit, picnic or play.
2.3	Return to the park entrance at the main trail and go over the bridge and turn left. Don't take the path to the left immediately out of Lake Artemesia; it ends in a few hundred yards.

2.9   Cross Berwyn Road. There is a small ice rink and playing field on the right.

3.1   Playground area.

3.3   Trail ends at 57th Avenue near Greenbelt Road. Retrace your path to return, for a total ride of 6.6 miles.

Indian Creek/Lake Artemesia

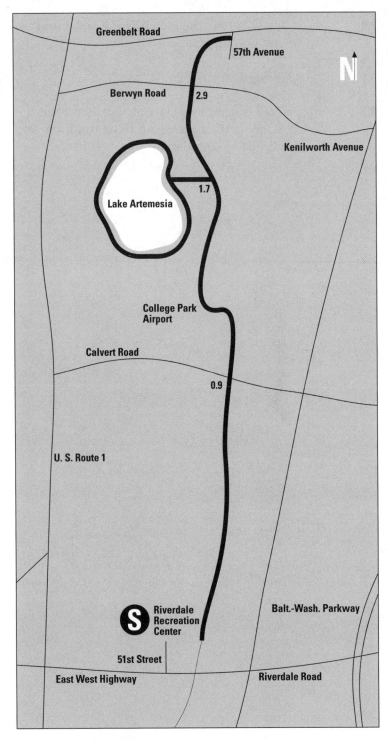

Paint Branch Stream Valley Park
2- and 4-mile tours

Another one of the growing number of stream valley parks, this short stretch of trail offers pleasant cycling along with numerous playgrounds and two public pools. At the starting point, historic Valley Mill is now a private residence with a picturesque covered bridge leading to the old mill house. Peter Kemp originally built the mill in the 1790s, and by the 1830s it had become the leading cornmeal producer in the country. The outdoor pool above the old mill house is open to the public during the summer for a nominal fee.

At the southern end of the trail, Martin Luther King Park has a large modern playground, a pond and exercise trail, and a public indoor pool open all year. The path to the park has a number of short hills; as you groan on the way up, think of how nice it will be to glide down the other side!

The best way to enjoy this trail is to pack a picnic lunch and leave it in the car at the parking lot on the north side of Randolph Road. Ride the Fairland path north and throw rocks in the ponds or swing on the swings. Then head south to Martin Luther King Park and spend a few hours there (there are several water fountains). Head back to the start and have a picnic or go swimming. Total length of the combined ride: about 5.5 miles.

Start:
Paint Branch Park, Fairland, Md. From Route 29 south from Burtonsville turn west on Randolph Road (south of Briggs Chaney Road). Park entrance is on your right.

Fairland Path (2-mile tour)

Miles	Directions
0.0	Take the asphalt path at the east side of the lower parking lot, next to the swimming pool.

0.2	Pond on left.
0.3	Go straight; the path going over the bridge on the right goes to a small pond and then ends at Serpentine Way. There is a small tot lot across Serpentine Way.
0.5	Bear right.
0.6	Cross basketball courts; go straight.
0.9	Reach Fairland Road. Going right on the sidewalk will take you to Old Columbia Pike and a gas station (.6 miles). Turn around to return to park.

Martin Luther King Park Path (4-mile tour)

Miles	Directions
0.0	Cross Randolph Road (carefully, this is a very busy road) and ride through the park parking lot.
0.2	Behind a steel gate the asphalt trail continues.
0.5	A self-guided nature trail follows the stream. The bike path begins a steep (but mercifully short) climb.
0.6	Bear left at the top of the hill; the path to the right goes into a local neighborhood.
1.2	After an exhilarating downhill ride (and some more uphill grinding), the path ends at Jackson Road. Ride a short distance on this quiet residential road and get back on the asphalt path on the right.

1.4 You are now entering Martin Luther King Park; bear right on the asphalt path and go along the baseball and soccer fields. A pond is straight ahead.

1.8 The path enters a wooded area, with many picnic tables. Head uphill to a fantastic playground. Retrace the path back for a total ride of about 4 miles.

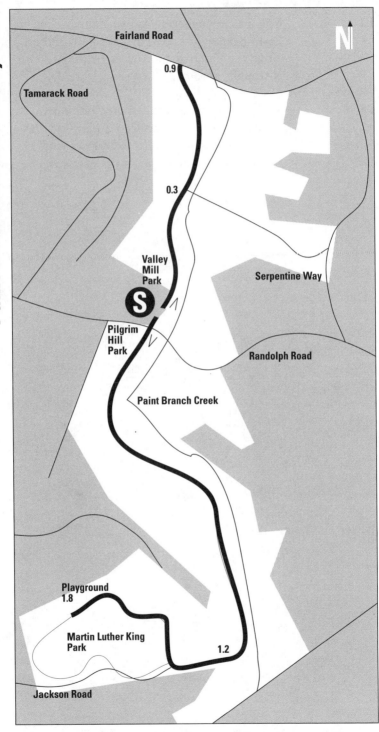

Paint Branch Stream Valley Park

Fairland Road

Tamarack Road

0.9

0.3

Valley Mill Park

S

Serpentine Way

Pilgrim Hill Park

Randolph Road

Paint Branch Creek

Playground
1.8

Martin Luther King Park

1.2

Jackson Road

N

Chesapeake and Ohio Canal Towpath
8- and 16-mile tours

The Chesapeake and Ohio Canal Towpath runs along the
Potomac River for nearly 185 miles, from Georgetown to
Cumberland, Md. First envisioned by George Washington in
the late 1700s, the C&O Canal was a massive engineering
feat that took over 20 years to build, finally reaching Cumberland in 1850. Long canal barges were pulled by mules,
and the canal level was raised and lowered using a system of
locks, much the same as those used in the Panama Canal.
While it continued to operate until 1924, the C&O turned a
profit only a few times in the 1870s. The canal lost the race
west to the railroads, and damage by frequent flooding
spelled the death knell for this magnificent ditch.

The canal was acquired by the Baltimore and Ohio Railroad and then sold to the U.S. Government in 1934. From
1934 to 1954, the towpath sat idle and fell into ruin. In
1954, the National Park Service proposed building a parkway along the towpath, modeled after Skyline Drive in Shen-
andoah National Park. This made a strange kind of sense in
the car-crazy 1950s, but luckily for hikers, cyclists and history buffs, Supreme Court Justice William O. Douglas cham-
pioned the preservation of the canal, even managing to get
the editors of Washington newspapers to walk the entire
length of the canal with him. The editors saw the light
(helped by the 50,000 canal enthusiasts who met them at the
end in Georgetown), and over the next 20 years the canal
was transformed into a long skinny park—paradise for cyclists.

There are people who have cycled the entire length of the
canal in one day—about 16 hours, as a matter of fact. A
more leisurely mini-vacation would be to go from Cumberland to Georgetown in four days, camping at the hiker/biker
campsites located every ten miles or so, or staying in hotels
at the towns a short distance away. For family day-trip cycling, just about anywhere along the canal is a fun place to
ride. The most popular destinations are the southern end at

Georgetown, Great Falls Park, Harpers Ferry and Paw Paw Tunnel to the west. I'll describe only one of the rides closest to Washington and a ride from Cumberland, which are our favorite areas to ride. However, stop in at the visitor's center at Great Falls Park and pick up one of the towpath guides and lay out your own routes.

Great Falls Ride (8-mile tour)

Cycling to Great Falls is a great way to beat the summer crowds and the $4 admission fee! Great Falls is where the Potomac makes its sharpest drop, and the dramatic views have made this area a popular day visit since the late 1700s. The river drops 41 feet in less than a mile, and there were six locks built along this stretch to raise and lower the canal barges. At the northernmost lock, the lockkeeper's house was enlarged twice by 1831 and became a popular hotel known as the Crommelin House. Later known as Great Falls Tavern, this magnificent old structure today houses the visitor center and canal history exhibits.

Recently restored bridges allow you to walk to Olmstead Island, where you will have spectacular views of the falls. These bridges were destroyed by Hurricane Agnes in 1972 but were recently rebuilt using funding by private contributions. You can buy tickets to ride in a restored canal barge pulled by mules and piloted by park personnel wearing authentic period costumes. There are picnic areas, a snack bar, rest rooms and several hiking trails. If you do walk or hike along the river, be very careful at the water's edge. The currents in this area are deceptively strong, and the rocks can be slippery and treacherous.

The ride described below begins a few miles south of Great Falls, at Carderock Park. There is no entrance fee, and there are many parking spots, along with rest rooms and water fountains. This makes for about an 8-mile loop, short enough to allow plenty of time to enjoy both Carderock and Great Falls. This section does contain one of the two unridable stretches of towpath between Georgetown and Cumberland, however. Just north of the Widewater area, less than a mile south of Great Falls, there is a stretch of rocks that requires walking or carrying bicycles. There is a detour on the berm side of the canal that is ridable, although quite rough.

This stretch is doable—but tricky—with a trailer. If you are not comfortable with your trailer, try this ride after you have gotten some experience.

Start:

Carderock Park. Take exit 41 from the Washington Beltway (I-495) west towards Carderock. Exit at the signs for Carderock, and turn left at the stop sign. Follow the park road, and after going under the bridge (actually a large culvert with the towpath passing overhead), turn right and park in the first parking lot on the right. If you turn left you will reach a parking lot that has access to the Billy Goat hiking trail. Great Falls Park telephone is 301-299-2026 (TDD: 301-299-3613).

Miles	Directions
0.0	From the parking lot, turn left onto the park road. After a few hundred feet there will be a footpath on the right leading through the trees to the towpath. It is a little bumpy, but wide enough to walk a bike and trailer through. When you reach the towpath, turn left and head towards Great Falls.
0.6	Reach bridge over canal; the Billy Goat hiking path access is on the left. If you enjoy hiking, this is a fun walk with great views of the river.
1.4	Reach the beginning of the Widewater section, a popular area for canoeists and kayakers. About a mile ahead the towpath is not ridable. If you are pulling a trailer or have small children on kiddie seats, turn right at the detour sign. Straight ahead are stairs leading to the detour path; or you can ride up to the right and turn left at the chain keeping cars off the detour path. If you are riding with older children who can walk their bikes, continue straight for two miles to reach Great Falls.

1.6	Ride on detour path. This is a wide but rough dirt road.
2.9	Reach bridge to towpath. Walk bikes over bridge, and turn right on towpath.
3.2	Path to falls overlook on left.
3.5	Great Falls Tavern and visitor's center on right.
3.7	Snack bar to the right. Retrace path to return to Carderock.

Cumberland Ride (16-mile tour)

One of the major goals of the Chesapeake and Ohio Canal was to reach Cumberland, Maryland, to begin shipping coal from mines in the hills of Allegany County to the population centers of the east coast. In 1850 the canal reached Cumberland and by 1870 canal boats moved nearly a million tons of freight. The Baltimore and Ohio Railroad had reached Cumberland in 1842, however, and the canal was never able to overcome the railroad's eight-year head start.

This section of the towpath is proof that the railroad is still king in Cumberland. As you pedal the nine miles from Cumberland to Iron Mountain, the ding ding of train bells and the thrum of powerful locomotives will rise above the sounds of the river. You will pass under a number of railroad bridges and ride alongside the enormous CSX switching yard. As you head south, you will see the Potomac River valley to your right and the railroad to your left. The view to the right is much prettier—railroads generate a lot of industrial strength trash. The towpath surface in this section is pretty rough. In places there are only wheel ruts. I do not recommend this ride for trailers, although I have done it with my daughter and we had a blast. Don't do this section if it has rained within the last week; you will think you are riding in the swamps of Borneo.

This ride begins at the Western Maryland Scenic Railroad station in Cumberland. An excursion train to Frostburg operates Tuesdays through Sundays from May through October. In November and December the train runs only on weekends. The train chugs uphill on a guided tour of the hills above Cumberland, about a 45-minute trip, with a 90-minute layover at the Old Depot Center. There are shops and a restaurant at the depot, and a huge turntable that will spin your locomotive around for the return trip. Back in Cumberland, you can visit the C&O Canal Information Center next to the railroad gift shop.

The bike ride ends at North Branch Park and canal lock 74, where there are picnic tables and paths along the river. At lock 75 there is a replica of a canal barge and a lock-keeper's house. Each summer C&O Canal Days are held at lock 75, with Civil War era reenactments, crafts, food and music. To return to Cumberland you can simply retrace your path along the canal, or if you want a shorter but hillier return route, you can take Route 51 back. This road has a wide, smooth shoulder for most of the return route, but there is some on-road riding.

Start:
Western Maryland Railroad Center, Cumberland, Md. Take exit 43C off I-68 in Cumberland. Follow signs to WMRR Center. Visitor center telephone is 301-777-5905.

Miles	Directions
0.0	From the Western Maryland Scenic Railroad station, ride to the left of the main building and ride under the highway overpass. The path is between the fence and the railroad tracks.
0.1	Cross over wooden bridge. Trail is on path to the right of the railroad tracks.
0.4	Go around gate. To your left are a number of CSX tracks.
1.0	Cross bridge.
1.5	Go around gate and continue straight on towpath.

1.6	Go under the first of many railroad bridges.
1.9	Cross road and continue on towpath.
2.7	Cross small driveway. Riverside Park on right.
3.9	Go over Evitt's Creek Aqueduct.
4.5	Hiker/biker campsite on right, with water and grill.
5.7	Cross road and continue on towpath.
6.1	Cross road and continue on towpath.
6.2	Cross road. Towpath continues to the right.
8.6	Continue straight on path.
8.9	Reach lock 75. The lockkeeper's house is on your right. During Canal Days, National Park Service staff man the house; there is not much to see otherwise. A small wooden bridge crosses the dry canal at the mouth of the lock and leads to a replica of a canal barge.
9.1	Reach lock 74 and North Branch Park. There are picnic areas and paths that lead to the river. To return you can turn around (for an 18.2-mile loop) or take Route 51 back to Cumberland for a 15.6-mile round trip. Route 51 has a wide, smooth shoulder for 5 of the 6.5 miles; the last 1.5 miles is on the roadway (there is a sidewalk). I don't recommend this road for small children or inexperienced cyclists.

9.2	If you are taking the road back, exit North Branch Park and turn left at River Road. Lock House Road to the right takes you smack into the rail yards.
9.4	Turn right at PPG Road, named for the Pittsburgh Plate Glass plant down the road a piece.
10.0	Turn left on Route 51. The first five miles are rolling hills with great views.
12.2	Impressive view of the CSX switch yard. The trains move pretty slowly through the yard and you can often race—and beat—50-ton locomotives.
13.7	Reach the outskirts of Cumberland and lose that nice wide shoulder. Traffic is not too bad in the right lane, or you can use the sidewalk.
15.3	Turn left at the sign for I-68 East.
15.5	Turn left on Howard Street.
15.6	Arrive at Western Maryland Railroad Station.

Chesapeake and Ohio Canal Towpath

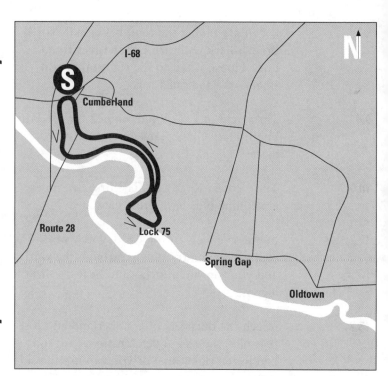

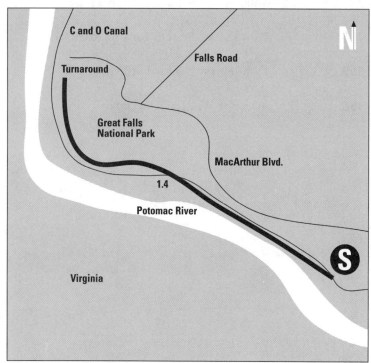

Henson Creek Stream Valley Park
5- and 7-mile loops

Running from Oxon Hill to Temple Hills in southern Prince George's County, this six-mile-long path is centered around the Tucker Road Community Park and Athletic Center. The park has tennis courts, a playground, a fitness trail, a fishing pond and an ice skating rink. Open during the winter, the skating rink has a hidden attraction: the pile of snow left behind the rink by the ice cleaning machine makes snowball fights possible throughout the season. North of the park, the trail passes through a small community park with an archery field and a commercial golf center, with miniature golf and driving ranges.

South of Tucker Road, the trail begins at the Tucker Road Community Center, with a modern playground, indoor recreation programs, and sand volleyball courts. The southern half of the trail ends at Oxon Hill Road, following the Henson Creek stream bed. This southern section is less travelled than the northern section, and the trail surface is not in as good condition, either. Avoid this section after heavy rains, unless you are in the mood for a mud bath. The foliage is spectacular in the fall, and this section is a delight for bird watchers.

Start:
Tucker Road Community Park. Take the Saint Barnabas Road (Route 414) west exit from the Capital Beltway. Turn left at John Hanson Lane and right at Saint Barnabas Road. Turn left onto Tucker Road and then left into the park.

North to Temple Hills (7-mile tour)

Miles	Directions
0.0	Start at the beginning of the fitness trail, to the left of the ice skating rink.

0.4	Turn right at the maintenance road and stay to the left of the yellow line.
0.6	Go through the parking lot, with the archery field to your left. Cross Bock Road to pick up trail again.
1.3	Cross two bridges, one with a rough gravel surface. Rosecroft Raceway is to the left across the stream.
2.2	Cross stream on bridge and begin slight uphill stretch.
2.5	The trail ends abruptly at Brinkley Road. Exit through the church parking lot to the left and turn right on Brinkley. On the right is a commercial golfing center with miniature golf and driving ranges.
2.7	Turn left through a small parking lot at the pumping station and pick up the trail again.
3.4	The trail ends at Temple Hill Road. Retrace your path to return.

South to Oxon Hill (5-mile tour)

Miles	Directions
0.0	Head out of the parking lot and cross Tucker Road onto the asphalt sidewalk on the south side of Tucker. Turn left (southeast).
0.2	Turn right on Ferguson Lane and right into the Tucker Road Community Center parking lot. Pick up the trail at the back of the parking lot. Nice playground and volleyball court here.

0.7	Continue straight on path; the path to the right goes to a local neighborhood (E. Barrett Road).
1.7	Cross bridge over stream.
1.9	Go under Indian Head Highway.
2.4	Pass through Tor Bryant Estates neighborhood park.
2.6	Climb uphill, trail ends at Oxon Hill Road. Retrace your path to return.

Henson Creek Stream Valley Park

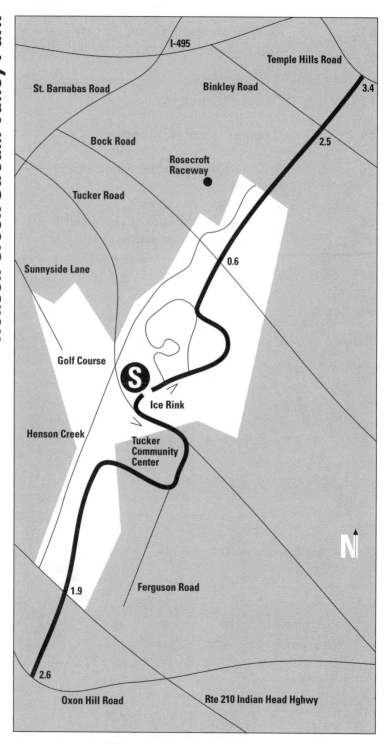

Columbia
15-mile loop

From a cyclist's point of view, both Columbia and Reston make good cases for planned communities. Established in the late 1960s, Columbia has developed an extensive network of bicycle trails. Most of the trails are short paths connecting communities with neighborhood centers and schools, but there is a "spinal system" of paths cutting diagonally across this Howard County town that makes for enjoyable family riding.

The down side to riding bicycles in Columbia is that it is easy to get lost—very easy. There are few trail signs, and with so many short connector trails it is easy to lose the main route. The Howard County Pathway map is quite detailed, however, and the up side is that with so many paths it is also easy to get back on track.

The 15-mile loop described below hits the four major lakes in Columbia: Centennial Lake, Wilde Lake, Lake Kittamaqundi and Lake Elkhorn. The mileage doesn't include circling all these lakes, so you can extend the trip if you like. You can also shorten the loop to about nine miles by starting at Columbia Town Center and saving Centennial Park for a separate trip. Along the way you will pass playgrounds every half mile or so, no two alike. There are numerous convenience stores, fast food restaurants and local shops. The Columbia City Fair is held each summer on Lake Kittamaqundi.

Centennial Park covers 325 acres, including a large lake where you can rent a rowboat, canoe or paddle boat. The snack bar is open April through October. You can also rent boats at Lake Kittamaqundi, even radio-controlled model boats.

Start:
Columbia, Md. For the full loop, start in the Centennial Park north parking lot. From Route 29 take Route 108 west to Columbia and turn north on Centennial Lane. The parking lot is on the right, about one-quarter mile north of

Route 108. The trail begins at the end of the parking lot, to the left of the tennis courts. For the shorter loop, start at the lakeside Town Center parking lot, across from Columbia Mall. Take Route 29 to the south entrance to Columbia. Turn right on Little Patuxent Parkway and park in the first parking lot on the right after the library. A footbridge connects the parking lot to Columbia Mall.

Miles	Directions
0.0	From the Centennial Park north parking lot, take the trail to the left of the tennis courts, near a small pavilion. Head down a steep hill and turn right when you reach the main path around the lake.
0.2	Cross wobbly pontoon bridge. Bear left on the main trail.
0.7	Reach the road to the park center buildings. To your left is a snack bar, rest rooms and boat rentals. To continue on the long loop, turn right on the road and head uphill to Route 108.
0.9	Cross Route 108 onto Ten Mills Road. The next mile or so will be sidewalk riding or, for more experienced riders, riding along low-traffic neighborhood roads.
1.0	Turn right on West Running Brook Road.
2.0	Wilde Lake is on your right. There is a trail that goes halfway around this picturesque lake, and it is a popular spot for radio-controlled boats.
2.1	Cross Little Patuxent Parkway on the crosswalk and turn right to follow the asphalt path into the woods.

2.6   Reach Lake Kittamaqundi, Columbia's show-piece. There are several good restaurants that aren't snobby about dress, particularly Clyde's outdoor deck service in the summer. Columbia Mall is accessible via a foot bridge behind Clyde's. Continue along lakefront, walking bikes down broad steps near the boardwalk that leads to the carillon chimes.

2.8   The asphalt path continues behind the white building to the right of the carillon chimes.

2.9   Bear left on the path to take the bridge over Route 29. The path to the right leads to the Howard County Library. Once over the bridge, you will climb (or walk) a steep hill. Once you've conquered that one, it is nearly flat for the rest of the way.

3.5   Cross Steven's Forest Road. The path continues to the left of the convenience store. The Oakland Mills village center has food, miniature golf and ice skating.

3.7   Do *not* go through the tunnel under White Acre Road. Bear left and go to White Acre Road. Take the sidewalk a short distance to Thunder Hill Road.

3.8   Cross Thunder Hill Road. The path continues on the right.

4.2   Reach Oakland Mills Road, turn left and cross Old Montgomery Road. The trail continues on the other side of Old Montgomery Road.

4.5   Cross Tamar Drive. The trail continues to the right of the Jeffers Hill school, adjacent to Old Montgomery Drive. Cut through the parking lot.

4.9 Cross Major's Lane.

5.1 Bear right, do not cross bridge.

5.5 Cross Old Montgomery Road. For the next mile or so it will be hard to believe you are in the middle of Howard County's biggest city.

5.8 Bear right over bridge.

6.5 Go through tunnel under Oakland Mills Road. The path circles up to road; turn right and continue on sidewalk.

6.9 Immediately past Christ Episcopal Church, which dates back to 1711, turn right on asphalt path.

7.1 Bear right over bridge.

7.2 Bear right over bridge.

7.4 The trail forks at the northern end of Lake Elkhorn. Bear left to circle around the lake, about a 1.5-mile loop. You will pass a recreation center open in the summer and several pavilions and fishing areas. There is also an exercise course and a boat dock. To continue on the 15-mile loop, bear right at this fork and go over the bridge.

7.6 Turn right from the main lake path onto the asphalt connector path.

7.7 For the next quarter mile, stay on the main path. It is impossible to give foolproof directions here, just don't turn at paths that lead into townhouse developments.

7.9 Bear left.

8.0	Reach Cradlerock Way. Turn left on sidewalk.
8.1	Cross Cradlerock Way at crosswalk. Path continues across street at end of crosswalk.
8.3	Turn right on path.
8.4	Bear left on path, going behind neighborhood pool. There is a convenience store on the other side of the pool.
8.6	Cross Cradlerock Way and turn right on sidewalk. The path continues to the left after a short ride on the sidewalk.
8.8	Cross Windhart Way.
8.9	Turn right to go over bridge under power lines.
9.0	Cross Farewell Road at crosswalk. There are directions stenciled on the path surface for the next several miles.
9.3	Bear left at playground.
9.4	Follow path through school parking lot. Reach Steven's Forest Road and turn right on sidewalk.
9.5	Continue on sidewalk, cross Kilimanjaro Road and then Santiago Road.
10.0	Reach Oakland Mills Village center and convenience store. Cross to the left at White Acre Road to return to path back to Columbia Town Center. You will now be whizzing down that hill you struggled up seven miles back.

10.5	Cross bridge over Route 29.
10.7	Retrace route along lakefront.
11.4	Cross Little Patuxent Parkway. Continue on sidewalk along West Running Brook Road.
12.5	Turn left onto Ten Mills Road.
12.6	Cross Route 108 and reenter Centennial Park. Follow park road to main building at lake. The trail continues to the right of the buildings.
12.8	Cross boat launching ramp.
13.4	Cross dam end of lake. Nice playground down hill to the right.
14.9	Return to original path connection. Walk bike up hill to parking lot.

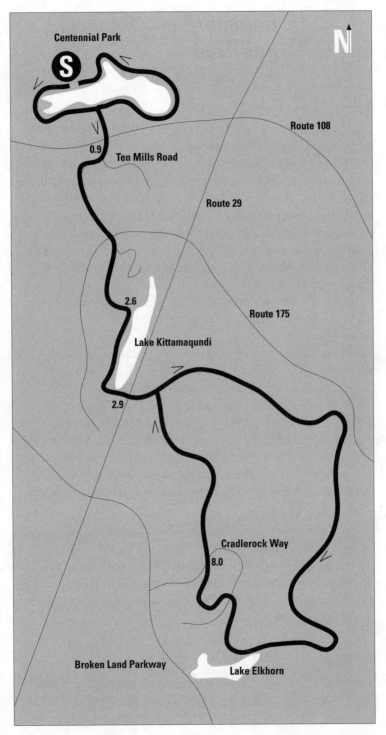

Columbia

N

Centennial Park

S

Route 108

0.9

Ten Mills Road

Route 29

2.6

Route 175

Lake Kittamaqundi

2.9

Cradlerock Way

8.0

Broken Land Parkway

Lake Elkhorn

Baltimore and Annapolis Rail Trail
17-mile tour

Operating under a variety of names, the Baltimore and Annapolis rail line carried passengers and freight from 1887 to
1968. At its peak, nearly two million passengers rode the B
and A between Maryland's capital and its largest city. In the
early 1900s, sleek electrified cars replaced the steam locomotives, featuring stained-glass windows, plush green seats, and
mahogany trim. The B and A was never very successful and
was given the nickname "Bumble and Amble." Rail opera-
tions shut down in 1968 and the track south of Dorsey
Road was abandoned in 1969.

Another shining example of rail to trail conversions, the
Baltimore and Annapolis Hike and Bike trail runs 13.3 miles
from Dorsey Road to Boulters Way, near Route 50. The trail
parallels Governor Ritchie Highway (Route 2) through
northern Anne Arundel County and provides easy access to
a wealth of services, while maintaining a rural look and feel
(especially on the southern half of the trail). The entire
length of the trail is well designed and fun to ride, but the
middle seven miles or so is the best area for family cycling.

A restored train station is used as a ranger station and interpretative center. There you can buy a very well designed
trail guide that is keyed to historical markers you will see
along the trail.

Start:

At the northern end of Harundale Mall, at Route 2 and
Dorking Road in Glen Burnie. If you want to start at the
southern end, park in the Park and Ride lot at Jones Station
Road and Route 2.

Miles	Directions
0.0	Start from the rear parking lot of Harundale Mall. The paved B and A trail cuts the park-ing lot in half. Believe it or not, this ordi-

nary-looking shopping center was the first enclosed, air-conditioned mall east of the Mississippi. Head south on the trail.

0.7	Cross Norfolk Road.
0.8	Cross bridge over Marley Creek. The original railroad bridge here was washed out by Hurricane Agnes in 1972, and an historic bridge transported from Missouri collapsed during the initial trail construction.
1.2	Crosswalk to Marley Station Mall. There you can find all the usual mall stuff.
1.5	Cross bridge over Route 100.
2.6	Pasadena Crossroads Mall on left.
2.8	Cross Jumpers Hole Road. Be careful, especially for cars turning from Elvaton Drive. This is a busy intersection.
2.9	Cross Jumpers Hole Road again. Grocery store on right.
3.2	Cross Waterford Road.
3.8	Cross West Pasadena Road. A bicycle shop is to your left a few yards ahead.
4.9	Cross Earleigh Heights Road, past the house with the sign that says "If you can't run with the big dogs, stay on the porch." A grocery store is on your left. The park ranger station and visitor center is on the right. There are rest rooms, a terrarium and nature exhibits in the ranger station, and you can buy maps and T-shirts. Immediately south of the ranger station is a wheelchair exercise course and a small nature preserve.

5.8	Cross Whites Road.
6.0	Cross McBrides Lane.
6.4	Cross Robinson Road.
6.8	Bike shop on left, trailer rental available. The brick building on the right is the original power station that provided electricity for the rail cars.
6.9	Cross McKinsey Road. The old Severna Park rail station is on the right, now the home of the Severna Park Model Railroad Club.
7.1	Cross Evergreen Road. The Severna Park library is across the street to the left.
7.6	Cross bridge over Round Bay Road.
8.3	Cross Hoyle Drive.
8.5	Arrive at Jones Station Road. The Park and Ride lot is across Baltimore Annapolis Boulevard to the left. A map on the left shows how to reach Anne Arundel Community College. Across Jones Station Road is the original power substation used by the railroad. The Anne Arundel Historical Society Browse and Buy Shoppe now occupies this building. For the 17-mile tour, turn around and follow the trail back to your car.

If you would like a longer ride, the trail continues south for 3.5 miles through secluded wooded areas. The trail ends rather abruptly at the Montessori School at Boulters Way, a stone's throw from the busy cloverleaf at the intersection of Route 2 and Route 50. The shoulder on Boulters Way is wide and smooth, and marked as a bicycle path. Seven-tenths of a mile south of the trail head, Boulters Way reaches Route 450 and a trail parking lot. While I do not recommend it when cycling with small children, Route 450 does have a decent shoulder for most of the three miles or so to Annapolis. One mile south of the Boulters Way parking lot you will reach a small picnic park on the banks of the Severn River. You can then ride on the sidewalk over the bridge and another mile to the public entrance to the Naval Academy. A short ride through the academy brings you to the public dock area of Annapolis, although the Naval Academy is worth a stop as well.

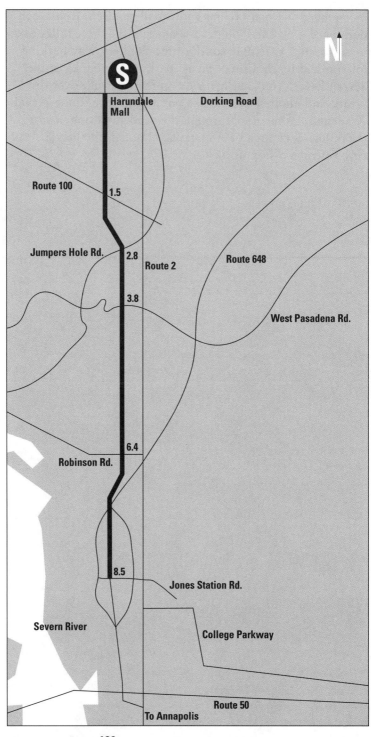

Baltimore/Annapolis Rail Trail

N

S

Harundale Mall

Dorking Road

Route 100

1.5

Jumpers Hole Rd.

2.8

Route 2

Route 648

3.8

West Pasadena Rd.

6.4

Robinson Rd.

8.5

Jones Station Rd.

Severn River

College Parkway

Route 50

To Annapolis

Quiet Waters Park
5-mile loop

Located in Anne Arundel county just south of Annapolis, this new 335-acre park is a real gem. There is a five-mile-long bicycle path, several foot paths, eight pavilion areas, an outdoor ice skating rink, a large playground and much more. Quiet Waters is an appropriate name; the park is so big and so well designed, it always seems as if you have the place to yourself. The park is closed on Tuesdays.

The visitor center has a restaurant, art exhibits and a rental center for in-line roller skates and, in the winter, ice skates. With its smooth asphalt paths and low traffic roads, Quiet Waters has become a popular destination and training ground for in-line skaters. A short foot path from the visitor center parking lot leads to a boat rental area on Harness Creek. Along the bicycle path you will find an exercise course, several playgrounds, several pavilions for under-cover picnicking, and a wetlands mitigation area. The south end of the park is nestled against the South River; the bicycle path leads to two gazebos that overlook the river, and stairs that lead to a promenade at river level.

There is an entrance fee of \$4 per vehicle for Anne Arundel County residents and \$6 per vehicle for nonresidents. If you park outside the park and walk or cycle in there is no charge.

Start:
From Route 50 east of the Washington Beltway, take the exit for Route 665, which will become Forest Drive after crossing Route 2. Travel 3.2 miles and turn right at Hillsmere Drive and the park entrance. Take the park road to the visitor center and bear right at the small pond. Park in the parking lot to the left of the Blue Heron Center. The trail begins at the back of this parking lot. Quiet Waters Park telephone number is 410-222-1777.

Miles	Directions
0.0	Start in parking lot I, to the right of the Blue Heron Center. Enter the trail at the rear of

the parking lot and turn left. Bicycles are not permitted on the path that goes straight; this leads to a composting demonstration area.

0.1 In about 100 feet turn right on the path, and then almost immediately turn left to follow the path.

0.2 Turn right on the path and follow it down a steep hill. Yes, you will have to climb back up this hill!

0.4 Turn right on the path at the Holly Pavilion.

0.9 Bear right on the path around the parking lot.

1.0 Turn right at the sign for the South River Promenade.

1.1 Arrive at a picturesque overlook of the South River, with several gazebos, benches and stairs down to river level. There is a bike rack to lock your bikes if you want to take a stroll along the river.

1.2 Follow path away from the promenade, and turn right on the path. You will go around a building that has rest rooms and soda machines. You will pass through a reforesting area. Those white tubes contain seedlings; the tubes are used to protect the slender saplings from deer.

1.8 Cross the park road and turn right on the bike path. That hill you enjoyed whizzing down now takes its revenge.

2.0 Cross the small road at the top of the hill and follow the path straight ahead to the right of the visitor center and the ice rink.

2.1	Turn right at the T in the path. A small pond and bridge is to your left. Cross the main park road and ride through the exercise course.
3.0	Cross the main park road and follow path.
3.5	Pass the Sassafras Pavilion on your left.
3.8	Cross several small wooden bridges.
4.0	Pass the Sycamore Pavilion and a small playground on your left.
4.1	The White Oak Pavilion is on your left. Going through the parking lot for this pavilion leads to the main park road and a large playground that is across the road. If you have small children, don't miss this playground.
4.5	Arrive back at the main parking lot.

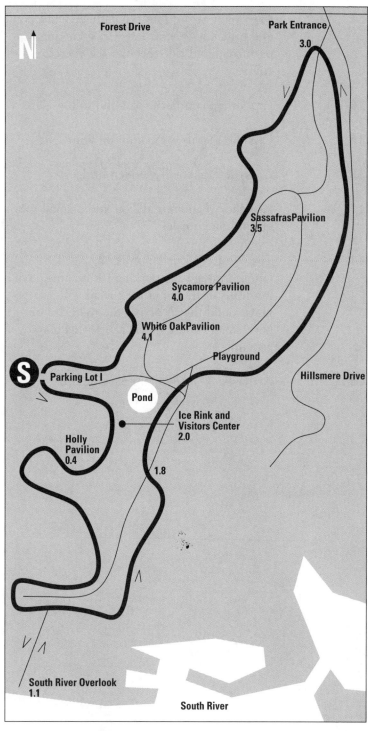

Quiet Waters Park

Forest Drive

Park Entrance
3.0

N

Sassafras Pavilion
3.5

Sycamore Pavilion
4.0

White Oak Pavilion
4.1

Playground

Parking Lot I

Hillsmere Drive

S

Pond

Ice Rink and
Visitors Center
2.0

Holly
Pavilion
0.4

1.8

South River Overlook
1.1

South River

Downs Park
5-mile loop

Located east of Severna Park on the Chesapeake Bay, Downs
Park is Anne Arundel County's northern oasis for family cycling. This 231-acre park has five miles of paved cycling
paths, a beach front for fishing and shell collecting, playgrounds, ponds and nature areas. There are also several
miles of hiking trails, including a .6-mile self-guided eco-
trail. You can pick up a guidebook and map at the Park Information Center for a small fee. Downs Park is closed on
Tuesdays.

Downs Park is located at the confluence of the Patapsco
River and the Chesapeake Bay, on a peninsula known as
Bodkin Neck. First settled in 1670, this area was farmed,
among others, by Charles Carroll, one of the signers of the
Declaration of Independence. In the early 1900s, H.R. Mayo
Thom, a wealthy Baltimorean, transformed the farmland
into a summer estate. In the mid seventies, Anne Arundel
County purchased the property, opening the park in 1982.
Several paved hiker/biker trails were built through the
woods, which feature groves of holly trees.

For part of the way the trail parallels the shoreline, providing views of freighters navigating the channel. There are
several amphitheaters where concerts and interpretative programs are held; there are also volleyball courts, baseball
fields and picnic areas. The paths are well marked and well
designed and a joy to cycle. Downs Park telephone is 401-
222-6230.

Start:

The park is located on Pinehurst Road, two miles north of
Gibson's Island. Take Route 100 east from Route 2. Route
100 runs into Pinehurst Road. Begin at the parking lot at the
Information Center. You can cycle into the park (and save
the admission fee) by parking at Bodkin Elementary School,
which you will see on your left. Ride east (to the left) on
Pinehurst for .5 miles (there is no shoulder) and you will see
the paved bike trail on the right. Ride for .4 miles on the
trail and you will reach the main entrance station.

Miles	Directions
0.0	Start at the Park Information Center next to the James Moore Memorial Overlook. Inside the Information Center you can see some enormous beehives and pick up a map. Follow the asphalt path around behind the Information Center to the perimeter path, which parallels the shore. Turn right and ride under the footbridge that leads to the overlook. For a quarter you can look through powerful binoculars from the overlook and check out sailboats and freighters on the bay.
0.2	Continue straight on path through holly trees.
1.3	Reach the main park entrance. Cross the park road—watch for traffic.
1.5	Cross the park road again. Immediately turn left on the path.
1.8	Return to the Information Center and go back to the Perimeter path. This time turn left on the path.
1.9	Bear right on the path, around the volleyball courts.
2.0	Bear right to go around the bay overlook.
2.1	A boardwalk and stairs leading to the pond are on your right. Follow the trail and turn right after the rest rooms.
2.4	Follow the path over the footbridge that crosses over Pinehurst Road.
2.5	Continue straight on path.
2.9	Path crosses over a creek.

3.0   Turn right on path. The path winds around Locust Cove and a natural area until it reaches several softball fields.

3.9   Cross Pinehurst Road and return to the main park entrance. At the entrance booth turn right on the path.

5.0   Continue straight on path.

5.3   Return to Information Center, with concession stand and playground on the right.

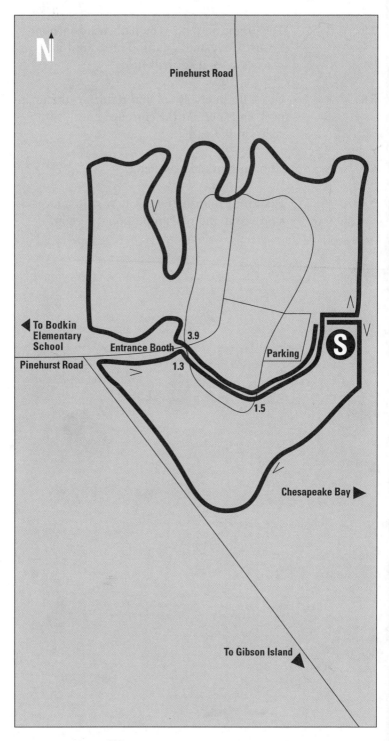

Oxford Ferry/St. Michael's
29-mile loop or 16-mile tour

St. Michael's is one of the most popular cycling destinations in Maryland. The terrain is table-top flat, and most of the roads have wide, smooth shoulders. St. Michael's is the home of the Chesapeake Maritime Museum, and more bed and breakfast hotels than you can shake a stick at. The museum and several restaurants overlook the picturesque harbor that was once a major shipbuilding area. Local history has it that when the British tried to bomb St. Michael's during the Revolutionary War, the town was blacked out and lamps lit miles away to simulate a town. The British gunners fell for the trick, and the town was saved. There are several boat tours that leave from the harbor, and there is a restored lighthouse you can tour.

The loop tour described below starts in Easton, home of the annual waterfowl festival held in November. At 29 miles, the loop is a little long for preschoolers and inexperienced cyclists. However, the loop breaks into three easy segments: Easton to Oxford, 9 miles; Oxford to St. Michael's, 8 miles; and St. Michael's to Easton, 11 miles. An alternative linear route (8 miles each way) is described below, as well, from Oxford to St. Michael's and back again. This takes advantage of the ferry ride and the two scenic towns and eliminates the least interesting sections.

Oxford is another old shipbuilding town on the eastern shore of the Tred Avon River. There is a ferry that will take you across the river to continue on to St. Michael's. The ferry runs from March 1 to mid December (when the St. Michael's Christmas festival is held) and costs $1.50 for cyclists. The ferry generally operates from 7 A.M. to sunset during the week (till 9 P.M. in the summer) and from 9 A.M. to sunset on weekends. Spend some time in Oxford; the shops are interesting and the food is good. The Robert Morris Inn is an attractive bed and breakfast that is very cyclist friendly.

Start:

YMCA, Easton, Md. Take Route 50 east from the Bay Bridge. Turn right onto Route 322 at Easton and then turn

129

left onto Route 333 at traffic light. The YMCA is on the right. Park at the right end of the parking lot, near the paddle tennis courts. For shorter Oxford–St. Michael's linear route, turn right on Route 333 from Route 322 and travel about nine miles to Oxford Community Center on left.

Miles	Directions
0.0	Turn left out of the YMCA parking lot.
0.1	Stay straight on Route 333, cross Route 322 at the light. The shoulder will be wide and smooth for most of the next nine miles.
2.0	Cross bridge over Peach Blossom Creek. Shoulder narrows over bridge.
3.5	Cross bridge over Tripp Creek. Shoulder narrows over bridge.
5.3	Grocery store on left.
8.8	Oxford Community Center on left; alternative starting point for 16-mile tour.
9.5	Take ferry across Tred Avon River; $1.50 for cyclists. At other end of river follow Bellevue Road. There are no shoulders, but traffic is generally light.
12.5	Turn left onto Route 329 at the Royal Oak store.
14.0	Turn left onto Route 33. This is a busy road, but the shoulder is wide and smooth.
16.8	Enter the outskirts of St. Michael's. The shoulder narrows and disappears here.
17.1	Turn right onto Mill Street at sign for Maritime Museum.

17.4	Arrive at the Maritime Museum and seafood restaurant in a lovely little cove.
17.8	Go back to Route 33 and turn left for return.
21.2	If you started at the Oxford Community Center, turn right onto Route 329 and re-trace the path back to the ferry. To return to Easton stay on Route 33.
21.6	Go over bridge over Oak Creek. Shoulder narrows over bridge but the bridge has finally been paved!
27.4	Turn right onto Route 322.
28.8	Turn left onto Route 333.
28.9	Arrive at YMCA.

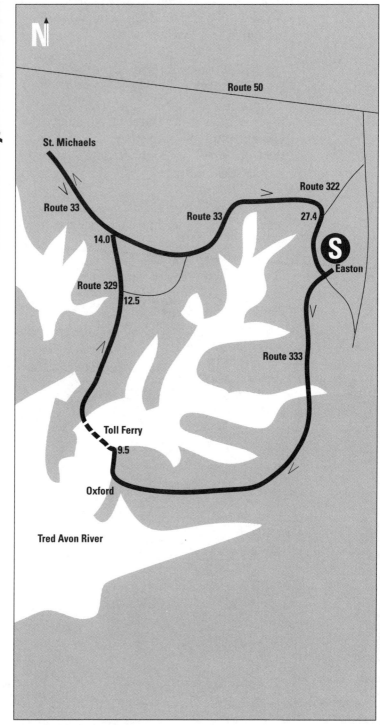

Oxford Ferry/St. Michaels

N

Route 50

St. Michaels

Route 33

Route 322

27.4

Route 33

14.0

S

Easton

Route 329

12.5

Route 333

Toll Ferry

9.5

Oxford

Tred Avon River

Washington and Old Dominion Rail Trail
8- and 14-mile tours

The Washington and Old Dominion Rail Trail was the first rails-to-trails conversion in the Washington area and has been so successful that it has been used as a model for many other such conversions across the country. Running 42 miles from Shirlington to Purcellville, the W&OD is one of the most popular trails in the country. At the eastern end in Shirlington, the W&OD connects to the Mount Vernon trail via the Four Mile Run bicycle path. Future plans are to continue the trail to Front Royal (and the Appalachian Trail) and to develop a connection with the C&O Canal Towpath via White's Ferry.

Built in 1859, the Washington and Old Dominion Railroad ran for over one hundred years, although it was almost destroyed in the Civil War. The railroad had its financial ups and downs, gradually shifting from hauling coal from the Appalachians to carrying vacationing Washingtonians to villages with romantic names such as Dunn Loring and Paeonian Springs. The rail line folded in 1968 and the Virginia Electric and Power Company bought the right-of-way, gradually signing it over to the Northern Virginia Regional Park Authority beginning in 1977.

The W&OD trail makes for fun riding anywhere along its 42-mile length. The best sections for family biking are along the ten-mile stretch encompassing Vienna, Reston and Herndon. Farther west the trail passes through Leesburg, which has a restored downtown area and several parks, and ends at Purcellville, where there are some fantastic local restaurants. For families with children, two attractive rides are described below.

The first ride covers an eight-mile loop at the eastern-most section of the trail. This ride starts near busy Shirlington but quickly dives into woodlands. There are several parks along the way, and you can also connect to the Four Mile Run bike path, which swoops up and down hills parallel to the relatively flat W&OD trail. It is a little tricky, but you can also head east from the start and connect to the Mount Vernon Trail south of National Airport. At the eastern end of this ride, you can also connect to the Custis Trail, which runs along I-66 to Rosslyn and Roosevelt Island.

Shirlington Tour (8 miles)

Start:
Take the Shirlington Road exit (exit 6) from I-395 south in Virginia. Bear right at the exit onto Shirlington Road; the trail begins at the intersection of Shirlington Road and Four Mile Drive. Park along the street or in the nearby shopping center. Washington and Old Dominion Railroad Regional Park telephone is 703-729-0596.

Miles	Directions
0.0	Start at the beginning of the trail at Shirlington Road.
0.6	Cross Walter Reed Drive.
1.2	Cross George Mason Drive.
1.7	Cross Columbia Pike.
2.1	The hiking trail into the woods on the right goes around a bog on a boardwalk. Great birdwatching—lock your bikes to a tree and walk.
2.2	Long Branch Nature Center is to the left.
2.3	Playground to the left.
2.4	Glencarlyn Park.
2.7	Go under Route 50, Arlington Boulevard.
3.0	Go under Springs Road. Trail comes out in the midst of a disc (as in Frisbee) golf course.

3.2   Go through Bluemont Park, with play-grounds and playing fields. Turn left on path after the parking lot.

3.4   Cross bridge, trail takes a sharp left.

3.6   Go under Wilson Boulevard.

4.1   Reach I-66. If you want a longer ride, turn right to connect to the Custis Trail, which is a great bicycling commuting route to Rosslyn and the Mount Vernon Trail (about four miles). For this shorter ride, simply retrace path to return, for a total round-trip of about 8 miles.

Vienna/Reston Ride (12 miles)

For most of this route, a horseback riding trail runs alongside and criss-crosses the W&OD paved path. The horse trail is much more rugged and is a popular ride for mountain bikers. Horses leave plenty of mementos along the path, so ride carefully.

There are playgrounds at both ends of this ride, with nature trails, streams and many old bridges in between. If you ride early in the morning, you are likely to see deer, foxes and other wildlife. There are restored railroad stations along the way, including one that houses an operating model railroad run by the Northern Virginia Model Railroaders. It is open to the public many Saturdays from 1 to 5 P.M. Call 703-938-5157 for details.

At the Reston end, you can connect with Reston's extensive system of paved paths. The Reston Visitor's Center is just off the path, and you can buy a map of the paths for $1. There are plenty of places to stop and eat, and there are several water fountains. There is very little shade along this stretch of the W&OD, so try and bring plenty of water or ride on cloudy or cool days. At the Vienna end, there are many restaurants and fast food places. Adjacent to the Vienna Community Center is a large, modern playground.

Start:

Vienna Community Center. Take Route 123 south from the Washington Beltway (I-495). After entering the town of Vienna, turn left at Park Street. The Vienna Community Center is ahead two blocks on the right. There is parking adjacent to the trail, next to the recycling center.

Miles	Directions
0.0	From the Community Center, turn right (west) on the path.
0.2	Reach Maple Street, Route 123. Turn right on the sidewalk to cross this busy road at the traffic light. When you have crossed, turn right on the sidewalk to return to the path. Turn left on the path.
0.5	Cross Dominion Street at the Freeman House. This majestic old house was built in 1859 and was used as a country store, post office and railroad station. It now houses a store and museum that is open on weekends. On your right is a bright red caboose, known as Vienna Caboose #503. This 30-ton car was built in 1948 and lovingly restored by many train buffs. You can climb up and peer in or look at the time capsule that won't be opened until the year 2040.
0.6	Cross Ayr Hill Road, with a restored train station on your left. This building now houses a model railroad system run by the Northern Virginia Model Railroaders. The trail now leaves this industrial park area behind.
2.4	Cross wooden bridge over Piney Branch.
3.1	Cross wooden bridge over Difficult Run. The path to the right leads to Tamarack Park, with a few picnic tables.

3.5   Cross Hunter Mill Road.

4.0   After short, steep hill, cross Buckthorn Lane. After going down hill on the other side of the road, the Twin Branches nature trail is on your left.

4.7   Cross Sunrise Valley Drive.

4.9   Go under Dulles Access Road bridge. The overpass is covered with fairly intelligent, PG-rated graffiti.

5.1   Cross Sunset Hills Road. Water fountain on right.

5.5   Cross Michael Faraday Drive.

5.6   Reach Wiehle Avenue. Fast food on right. The Reston Visitor's Center is located in Isaac Newton Square. Buy a map and explore Lake Anne or Lake Newport. Lake Fairfax County Park is a short ride away, as well. Retrace trail to return to Vienna.

Washington and Old Dominion Rail Trail

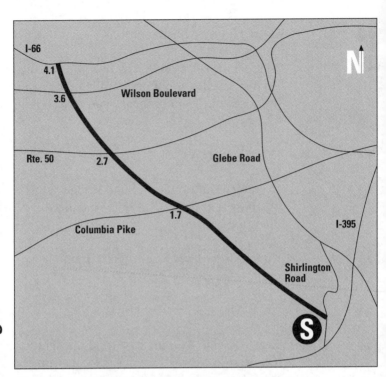

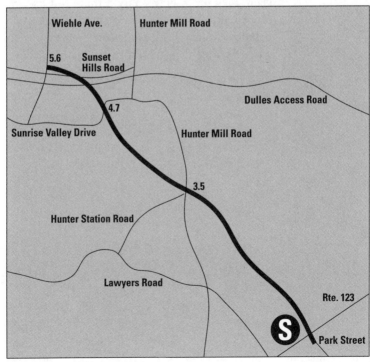

Accotink Trail
9-mile tour

I call this the mini–mountain bike tour. It is definitely not for trailers, since most of the trail is rough, packed dirt with many ruts, roots and bumps. It is a popular ride for mountain bikers and it is a great introductory ride for young mountain biker wannabees. The trail connects Wakefield Recreation Center with Lake Accotink Park, which are both fun spots to bring children.

Wakefield Recreation Center has baseball fields, picnic areas, basketball and tennis courts, an indoor recreation center, and the intriguing Gamefield Jogging Course. This is a much more interesting version of the standard exercise course, with many more stops with imaginative activities at each stop. The path is a little too narrow, and too busy, for safe cycling, but kids will have fun running through the trail stations. A maintenance road leads north from the Recreation Center, connecting with a local bike trail that goes to a pedestrian overpass that crosses the Washington Beltway.

At the southern end, Lake Accotink Park is 450 acres of green space in the middle of one of the fastest-developing areas in northern Virginia. The park rents canoes, rowboats and paddleboats and has pontoon boat rides as well. There is also a small miniature golf course (no, I am not being redundant, it really is tiny) and an old-fashioned carousel. There are several playgrounds and picnic areas as well. The Southern Railroad passes just south of the lake on a gaily painted bridge. These tracks once carried the Orange and Alexandria rail line, which began service in 1851.

Start:
Wakefield Park. Take Braddock Road west from the Capital Beltway (I-495) and take the first right onto Queensbury Avenue. Park in the first parking lot on the left at the trail head, or you can park half a mile down Queensbury at the Recreation Center and follow the asphalt path along the baseball fields to the start of the trail.

Miles	Directions
0.0	The trail begins at the north end of the parking lot next to the baseball fields. Look for the sign for the Wakefield Accotink Trail, a packed dirt trail that immediately leads over a small wooden bridge.
0.4	Bear right to go under Braddock Road. Bear right on path after you go under the bridge, around perpetually muddy area to small bridge.
0.7	Continue straight on path.
1.9	Bear right over small stone bridge.
2.0	Climb small hill to nice views of Lake Accotink and beginning of exercise course.
2.1	Go down short steep hill to wooden bridge, with short killer climb back up the other side. Beware of wet leaves on the path and bridge.
2.3	Bear right to follow path along the lake shore.
2.5	Cross bridge to marina and boat rental area. Carousel is straight ahead, with picnic areas and playground across the parking lot. After playing miniature golf, or riding the carousel, or renting a boat, you can turn around and head back to Wakefield or continue along the park road behind the marina. At the park information building, a loop trail is marked that goes around the lake. Since it contains an on-road stretch, I haven't included the loop here. Ask park personnel for details. A paved trail will lead off to the right as you near the railroad bridge.

2.8	Cross small stone bridge behind the Lake Accotink dam. (This bridge is sometimes under water. If so, turn around here for a five-mile ride). A short, steep uphill climb follows. This hill is a walker-upper for my age bracket.
2.9	Turn right, follow trail along lake shore.
3.9	Continue straight on trail at trail sign.
4.4	Reach park gate, where after a short on-road stretch you can continue to loop around the lake if you got directions at the marina. Return back by retracing trail, for a total ride of about nine miles.

Accotink Trail

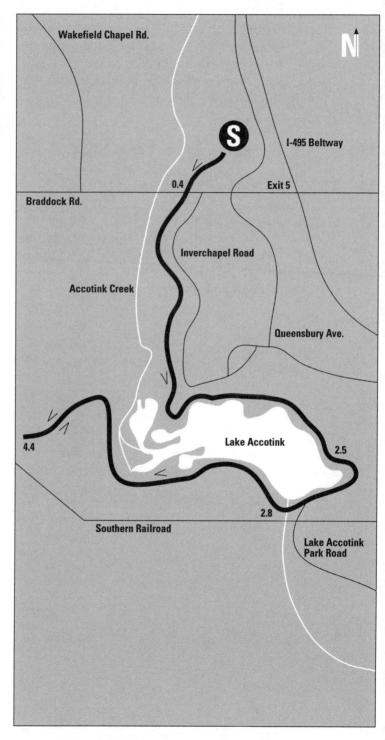

Burke Lake
5-mile loop

Burke Lake is a small oasis in the heart of suburbia. Along with a superb hiking/biking trail, Burke Lake Park offers boat rental, a miniature railroad, an old-fashioned ice cream parlour, playgrounds, picnic areas and a disc (Frisbee) golf course. There is also a real golf course adjacent to the park, with a driving range as well. The lake is a popular fishing spot for bass and muskie. There is a $4 admission fee during most of the year if you are not a Fairfax County resident.

The hiking/biking trail winds around most of the lake, hugging the shore and offering great views for its entire length. The trail sort of disappears between the marina area and the playgrounds, so I tend to use the park road for a short stretch. There is not much traffic on these roads, but be careful on summer weekends. The trail is popular with joggers, walkers and bikers. Stay to the right on the trail, yield to pedestrians, and give warning when you are going to pass. Foot traffic can be quite heavy, especially on the stretch along the miniature railroad.

Start:
Burke Lake Park in Burke, Va. Take Route 123 south from Route 66. South of George Mason University, cross Burke Lake Road. Turn left into the park immediately after passing golf course on left.Continue straight and follow signs for the marina parking lot.

Miles	Directions
0.0	Follow park road west from the marina parking lot, back towards park entrance.
0.1	Turn left on road towards picnic areas.
0.4	Playground and rest rooms on left, continue on road.
0.6	Another playground. Continue straight.

0.9	Take trail to the right through woods to parking area and boat launch area. Wide gravel path continues through woods along lake across the boat ramp.
1.4	After passing over earthen dam at southern end of lake, bear left on main gravel trail.
2.7	After riding through alternating stands of holly and pines, bear left on gravel trail.
3.6	Continue straight on trail, nature trail goes off to the right.
4.2	Short stretch on the shoulder of the park loop road. Immediately after crossing bridge, turn left to get back on trail.
4.6	After paralleling the miniature railroad tracks for a while, continue straight on trail at the teeny-tiny railroad station.
4.8	Continue straight on trail, amphitheater on right.
5.0	Disc golf course on right. Trail loops along shore.
5.1	Bear left to go back to parking lot.
5.2	Return to marina parking lot.

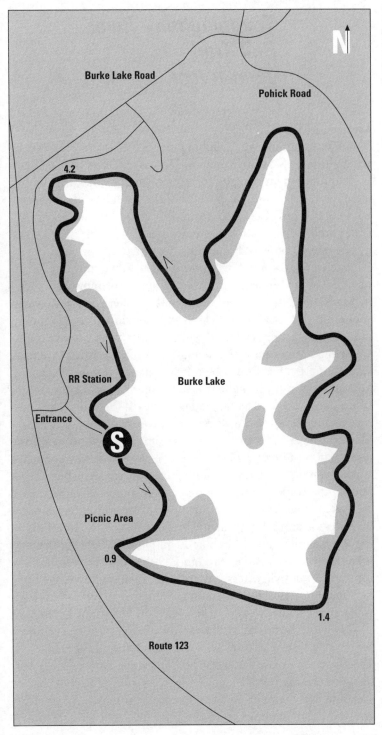

Burke Lake Road

Pohick Road

N

4.2

RR Station

Burke Lake

Entrance

S

Picnic Area

0.9

1.4

Route 123

Youghiogheny River Rail Trail
22-mile tour

Located in Western Pennsylvania, approximately 200 miles
from Washington, the Youghiogheny River is not really in
the Baltimore-Washington area. However, Deep Creek Lake
is a popular vacation spot for area residents, and it is only a
45-minute ride from Deep Creek Lake to the Youghiogheny
River Rail Trail. Centered around Ohiopyle State Park, this
trail could be a vacation destination all by itself.

The Youghiogheny River runs north from Maryland into
Pennsylvania, joining the Monongahela River south of Pitts-
burgh. The upper section of the "Yough" (pronounced yock)
in Maryland boasts some of the most challenging whitewater
rapids on the East Coast. The Rail Trail runs from Connels-
ville, Pennsylvania, to Confluence, Pennsylvania, where the
Casselman River joins the Yough. The section from Connels-
ville to the Bruner Run take-out (about seven miles from
Ohiopyle) is still a rough surface, in many places consisting
of the large stones used as ballast beneath the rails. The
seven-mile section from Bruner Run to Ohiopyle has a usa-
ble surface, but it is the ten miles from Ohiopyle to Confluence that is the real gem.

At the start in Ohiopyle State Park you can rent bicycles
and kiddie trailers from a number of commercial outfits, as
well as arrange whitewater rafting trips or go hiking on over
40 miles of day hiking trails. The park is also the terminus
for the 70-mile Laurel Highlands hiking trail. During the
main season from April through October the community
center in Ohiopyle offers day care for small children at very
reasonable rates. There are several miles of mountain bike
trails at the southern end of the park on Sugarloaf Knob.

This route begins at a renovated railroad station that now
serves as a visitor center. You will ride south along the
Youghiogheny on a level, crushed limestone surface. You are
likely to see the telltale signs of beavers along the trail. If
you ride early enough in the morning, you may have to clear
gnawed-down saplings from the trail. You will also see the

remains of the Western Maryland Railroad that worked the southern side of the river. The CSX tracks on the north side of the river are still active carrying coal and other freight.

There are several places to eat at the Confluence end of the trail, with the River's Edge Cafe being the cream of the crop. Have a pitcher of lemonade on the veranda and watch canoeists and ducks paddle down the river. Downtown Confluence is a few miles away; it is not worth the trip.

While a 22-mile roundtrip may seem too long when bringing small children, we have found that this ride is perfect for our two-year-old daughter. If you start at about 10 A.M. you will arrive at the lunch stop somewhere between 11 and 11:30. An hour or so for lunch, and the ride back hits right at nap time. Lauren usually sleeps for at least half of the hour-long ride back. The return trip is also downhill, so small children riding their own bikes will have an easier time as well.

Start:

Ohiopyle State Park, Ohiopyle, Penn. From I-68 in Keyser, Md., take the exit for Route 40 West. At Farmington, take Route 381 north to Ohiopyle. Park at the visitor center in the renovated railroad station just before the railroad bridge. Ohiopyle State Park telephone is 412-329-8591.

Miles	Directions
0.0	Start at Ohiopyle Visitor's Center in renovated rail station.
1.6	The trail splits from the river for a while. The silence is deafening when you lose the roar of the rapids.
2.5	A metal guardrail on the left marks a mandatory photo opportunity, as the river makes a sharp bend marked by some major riffles. To the right of the path is a small waterfall, the first of many.

3.5	Someone spent a lot of time building the stone fence on the right in the middle of no-where. Of course, that somebody had to do something with all the rocks they removed when they built the rail line.
4.3	In a small clearing on the left are benches and a path to the river.
7.0	After heavy rains or snow melts, the cliff face on the right sports a beard made of many small waterfalls.
8.7	Reach the Ramcat parking area, a popular put-in for rafting expeditions. Rest rooms and paths to the river are available.
8.8	Cross road. The spacing between the guard posts is very narrow. Be very careful if you are pulling a trailer.
9.4	Cross road. Again, the spacing between the guard posts is very narrow. Be very careful if you are pulling a trailer.
9.8	The trail ends at the road. Turn left on this quiet road and enjoy a nice downhill run.
10.3	Go under railroad bridge.
10.4	Turn left and go over the metal bridge. Be careful: This is not a busy area but many trucks do use the bridge.
10.5	At the end of the bridge, turn left onto River Road. If you continue straight you will go to the heart of Confluence. There is no there there, to paraphrase Gertrude Stein.

10.7   Arrive at River's Edge Cafe, a great place to eat lunch. This bed and breakfast is very cyclist-friendly and there is a bike shop next door. Don't forget to save some bread for the ducks along the river bank. Retrace your path to return, for a total ride of about 22 miles.

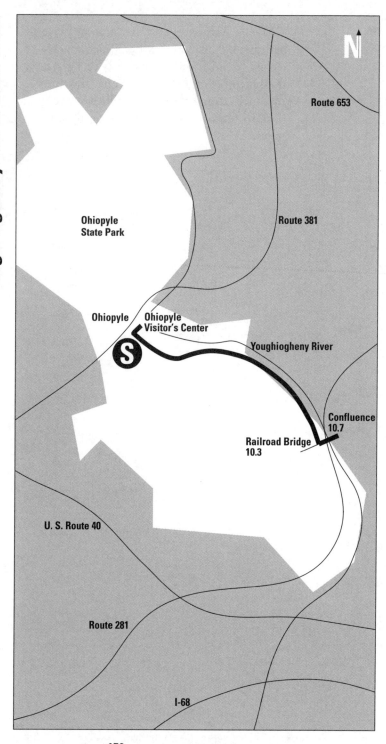

Youghiogheny River Rail Trail

Route 653

Route 381

Ohiopyle State Park

Ohiopyle
Ohiopyle Visitor's Center

Youghiogheny River

S

Confluence
10.7

Railroad Bridge
10.3

U. S. Route 40

Route 281

I-68

Blackwater Refuge
7-mile loop

Managed by the U.S. Fish and Wildlife Service, Blackwater
Refuge was established in 1963 as a refuge for migratory
waterfowl. Covering over 17,000 acres, the refuge is a stopping point for over 30,000 geese and 15,000 ducks each
year. Most of this land was originally run as a fur farm,
with trapped muskrats providing the fur for whatever it was
they did with muskrat fur in the old days. Today the open
water and dense woodlands are home to otters, opossums,
red foxes, muskrats and deer. Blackwater is also home to
several endangered species, including the bald eagle and the
peregrine falcon.

Blackwater Refuge is located just south of Cambridge,
Maryland, along the western side of Maryland's Eastern
Shore. The roads around the refuge are flat and lightly trav-
eled, making for fine cycling. Within the refuge, the five-
mile-long Wildlife Drive makes for a fun hour or two of cycling and bird watching. There are few amenities at Blackwater. The visitor center has nature programs and exhibits
and a panoramic view of the wildlife area. There are two
hiking trails along Wildlife Drive and several rest rooms.
There are no playgrounds or parks; Blackwater has truly
been designed for wildlife.

Unless you are a really avid birdwatcher or your kids are
studying Maryland's wildlife, Blackwater is too far a drive
solely for a cycling trip. However, if you are coming back
from Ocean City or doing the Easton/Oxford loop in this
book, Blackwater is a nice place to visit, pedal in and relax
in. November is the peak duck and goose migration period
and it is an amazing sight to see. The directions below are
for a seven-mile loop through the refuge, but a map for a
longer, 27-mile ride through the surrounding area is available at the visitor center. Since there are not always shoulders on the longer loop, I do not recommend it for small
children or inexperienced cyclists.

Start:

Take Route 50 east from the Bay Bridge. After passing
Cambridge, turn right onto Route 16 at signs for Blackwater
Refuge. At Church Creek, turn left onto Route 335. Turn left
onto Key Wallace Drive. Turn right into visitor center.
Blackwater Refuge telephone is 410-228-2677.

Miles	Directions
0.0	Exit visitor center parking lot towards Key Wallace Drive.
0.1	Turn right onto Key Wallace Drive.
1.3	Bear right on road and follow signs to Wildlife Drive.
1.7	Turn right onto Wildlife Drive. There is a $1 per bicycle fee, collected using the honor system.
2.0	Bear left, follow signs towards Marsh Edge trail.
2.1	Reach parking area for Marsh Edge walking trail. Trail leads to nice views of the wetlands. To continue loop, retrace route from trail area.
2.2	Bear left on road.
2.4	Road dead-ends. The observation tower is no longer here, but this is a great viewpoint area. To continue, backtrack on road.
2.7	Turn left on road.
2.8	Turn left on Wildlife Drive. Endangered squirrel crossing signs.
3.6	Woods Trail parking area on right. This trail is not very exciting, but there are some remains of an old steam shovel along the trail.

5.0	Turn left to follow Wildlife Drive. If you are all marshed out, you can go straight and then turn right on Key Wallace Drive to return to the visitor center. This will shorten the trip by about two miles.
6.2	Reach Route 335, turn right and ride on shoulder for short distance.
6.3	Turn right on Key Wallace Drive.
7.1	Turn right into visitor center parking lot.
7.2	Return to visitor center.

Blackwater Refuge

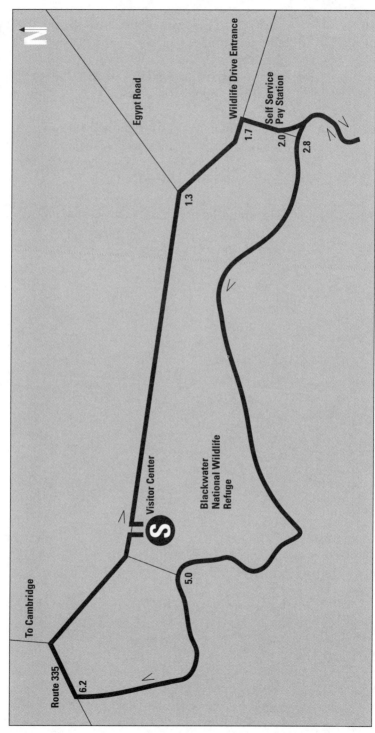

Chincoteague
11-mile loop

This beautiful island was known to the Indians as Gingo-
teague, or Beautiful Island. European settlers first lay claim
to the area in 1671, and the island was used mainly as a
livestock range throughout the 1700s. Protected from the Atlantic Ocean by Assateague Island, today the town of Chincoteague serves mainly as a resort area for visitors to the
Chincoteague National Wildlife Refuge (which is actually on
Assateague Island) and NASA's nearby Wallops Island facility.

The Chincoteague National Wildlife Refuge is for the
birds—literally. While we sometimes think that the ecology
movement began in the 1960s, the Chincoteague Refuge was
actually established in 1943 as a wintering area for migratory waterfowl. During the early 1900s the waterfowl popu-
lations that migrated to the Delmarva area were being devas-
tated by mass gunning of geese and ducks and massive
conversion of wetlands to farms and residential developments. Today the refuge is home to unusual birds such as
peregrine falcons, snowy egrets, dunlins and widgeons, as
well as herons, geese and ducks.

Chincoteague has also become famous for its herds of
wild ponies. Local legend has it that sometime in the 16th
century a Spanish galleon sunk off Assateague Island and its
cargo of mustangs swam safely to shore. During the 17th
century local landowners grazed their horses on the island to
avoid mainland taxes. Today the ponies are wild animals
that are used to the presence of humans but are by no means
domesticated. Quoting from the National Park Service brochure: "While usually appearing docile, they are prone to
unpredictable behavior and can inflict serious wounds both
by kicking and by biting. Do not feed or pet the ponies."
Your best bet to see ponies from a safe distance is from the
Woodland Trail.

Chincoteague is about a three- to four-hour drive from the
Washington-Baltimore area, too far for a day trip. There are
so many things to do there, however, it makes a great week-

end minivacation, especially in the spring and fall when the summertime crowds are gone. From June through October there are guided evening cruises on tour boats along Assateague Channel, and from April through November you can take a guided safari ride through the back roads of the refuge. Most area services are open from Easter to Thanksgiving; during the winter you will have the place to yourself. From Thanksgiving to New Year's, the refuge has periodic hunting openings that close several of the trails; call ahead if you plan to visit in December. The NASA Wallops Flight Facility is open free to the public year-round (Thursdays through Mondays from Labor Day to July Fourth, every day during the rest of the year). There you can see rocket launches and take guided tours of the facility.

The bicycle loop described below mixes trails with some of the refuge roads for a pedal-powered safari-like ride. You will ride around Snow Goose Pool on a road that is closed to cars every day until 3 P.M., and you will see thousands of birds of every size, shape and color. You'll then loop over to the Woodland or Pony Trail and from there to the Tom's Cove area at the sand dune line, where you can hike, fish or swim. It is almost always windy at Chincoteague, so you are guaranteed a headwind at least half the way. Of course, as an experienced cyclist you know by now that you will always be riding into a headwind.

Several places in the town of Chincoteague rent bicycles, so you can make a vacation of it without dragging along all those bikes. The Sea Hawk Motel, Piney Island Country Store, and T&T Rentals are a few that have bicycles for rent. Several of the bed and breakfast inns and hotels have bicycles available for guest use.

Start:

Chincoteague Chamber of Commerce. From the Bay Bridge, take Route 50 East to Salisbury, Md. Exit onto Route 12 south towards Snow Hill. Continue on Route 12 south until the Virginia border, where it turns into Route 679 shortly after the town of Stockton. Route 679 ends at Route 175; turn left and head towards Chincoteague. Immediately after passing over the bridge, turn left onto Main Street and then right onto Maddox Boulevard. The Chamber of Commerce is at the center of the first traffic circle you come to. The Chamber of Commerce telephone number is 804-336-6161. The Chincoteague National Wildlife Refuge telephone number is 804-336-6122.

Miles	Directions
0.0	Head east on Maddox Boulevard from Chamber of Commerce building in the middle of the traffic circle.
0.5	Crosswalk for bicycle path to north side of road.
0.7	Bridge over channel, signs explaining ecosystem on left.
1.0	Entrance station, pass over bicycle counter.
1.2	Enter visitor center parking lot. Visitor center on right. To continue, go through parking lot to the left.
1.3	Wildlife Loop Road, turn left at end of parking lot. Bear right on loop road. Cars are not allowed on this road before 3 P.M. You will circle Snow Goose Pool and probably have to avoid ducks, geese and heron as you cycle.
1.8	After following loop along water's edge, turn right onto Black Duck Trail.
2.7	Cross road to entrance to Woodland Trail.
2.9	Reach Woodland Trail entrance area. This trail makes a ice 1.6-mile loop through the area where the ponies are often found. There is an overlook area as well.
4.5	Return to entrance area and head back to park road.

4.7	Turn right on park road. Nice water views on both sides of road.
5.8	Turn right at small traffic circle in front of dunes.
6.0	Tom's Cove walking trail on right. You can lock bikes to the split-rail fence if you want to take a hike.
6.6	Reach end of road at sand where off-road vehicle area begins. Bicycles are not allowed in this area. Turn around and retrace road back to traffic circle area, or lock your bikes and take a walk along the shore.
7.3	Go straight through traffic circle; visitor center and bath house on right.
7.5	Trail straight ahead parallels dunes, with marshland on left.
8.8	Rejoin Wildlife Loop Road. Turn right on road.
9.0	Snow Goose overlook path. Bike rack for locking bikes if you want to walk the short path to the overlook. It is well worth the trip.
9.9	Boardwalk to overlook on left.
10.5	Turn right to return to visitor center, or go around the loop again (3.2 miles).
10.6	Return to visitor center. If you ride to the left of the visitor center onto the park road and turn left, in .2 miles you reach the lighthouse trail. A short walk brings you to the lighthouse where there are often art exhibits in the old oil shed.

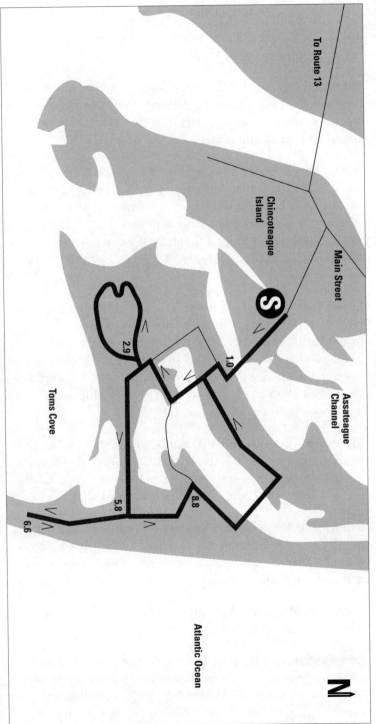

To Route 13

Chincoteague
Island

Main Street

Assateague
Channel

S

2.9

1.0

Toms Cove

5.8

8.8

6.6

Atlantic Ocean

N

There just wasn't room or time to include every ride, so here are a few that just didn't make the cut:

Reston. Like Columbia, Reston has an extensive, and very confusing, network of trails. Although much of the system is sidewalk, there are many nice paths connecting playgrounds, shopping centers and parks.

Bowie. This booming town in Prince George's County was one of the early leaders in building bicycle paths. After a construction boom in the seventies, however, attention moved to roads and other more mundane needs. The path along Route 197 and the shoulders of Route 301 are good transportation routes, and there are several neighborhood trails, as well.

Savage Park. Located off Route 1, a few miles north of Laurel, Maryland, this nature area runs along the middle branch of the Patuxent River. There is a 1.5-mile Historic Mill Trail, suitable for bicycles and strollers, that parallels the river and passes by the Bollman Truss Bridge and several stone dam abutments. The adjacent Savage Mill shops have a nice eatery, and a park is nearby.

Gettysburg. There are miles of roads suitable for cycling in the Gettysburg Battlefield National Park, although it is very hilly. Each year the Gettysburg Adams County Area Chamber of Commerce sponsors a ride through the battlefield.

Bull Run/Occoquan Parks. There are five miles of bridle paths that wend through hundreds of acres of bluebells. There are also playgrounds, campsites, a disc golf course, miniature golf and a swimming pool.

Ocean City, Maryland. There are several miles of boardwalk where cycling is allowed in the early mornings.

Arlington County. Arlington County, Virginia, is the most cycling-progressive county in the Baltimore-Washington area. There are 36 miles of off-road bike paths in Arlington County, including the Custis Trail, a popular commuting route that parallels I-66. Their bikeway map shows a 17-mile loop that is a fun ride, much of which is described in this book under the Mount Vernon and W&OD rides.

Carroll and Frederick Counties, Maryland. Both counties have put out bicycling tour maps, which cover hilly, on-road routes.

Coming Soon to a Trail Near You

There are a lot of new trails that are under construction or in the planning stages. Maybe the next edition of this book will be able to include:

Capital Crescent Trail. This 11-mile trail will connect Bethesda to Georgetown following the route of the old Georgetown spur rail line. It will provide an alternative to Rock Creek Park and allow loop rides using Rock Creek, the C&O Canal Towpath and the Capital Crescent. Construction began in early 1993.

Anacostia Headwaters Trail. Funding was approved in late 1992 for construction of a trail system that will connect the Northeast Branch Trail and other Prince George's County trails into a cohesive system.

Metropolitan Branch Trail. Paralleling the Metro tracks from Union Station to Takoma Park, the Metropolitan Branch Trail will connect downtown D.C. to the Sligo Creek trail system, as well as other local trails. This will be a component of the East Coast Greenway, a planned collection of trails that will connect Washington with Boston.

Baltimore Annapolis Trail Extension. Plans are being developed to extend the B and A Trail north of Dorsey Road.

Northern Central Rail Trail Extension. This is moving very slowly, but one day the NCRR Trail will reach York, PA.

Washington and Old Dominion. Not much progress, but there has been a lot of talk about extending this popular rail-trail to Front Royal, as well as providing a connection to the C&O Towpath via White's Ferry.

Resources

Other Guidebooks

. . . .

This trail guide concentrates on off-road trails that are relatively flat and free of traffic. As you and your family become more experienced cyclists, you may want to try some more challenging rides. The best cycling guidebooks for this area that I have found are:

Chesapeake and Ohio Canal Official National Park Handbook. National Park Service. This colorful guide details the history of the canal and provides a guide to recreation along the length of the towpath.

Chuck and Gail's Favorite Bike Rides. by Chuck and Gail Helfer (Cycleways Publications). Cycleways has several regional guidebooks out, but this one has the best rides in it.

Greater Washington Area Bicycle Atlas. by Charles Baughman, Bonnie Nevel and Bill Silverman (PAC/AYH, WABA). This is the grandaddy of all area cycling guidebooks, and for challenging, scenic rides it is the best.

Touring the Washington, D.C., Area by Bicycle. by Peter Powers (Terragraphics). This checkbook-sized guide has an unusual format that provides a simulated three-dimensional picture of each ride, spotlighting hilly areas and really giving you a feel for each ride. The directions are a little sparse, though, and most of the rides are hilly and on-road.

Towpath Guide to the C&O Canal. by Thomas Hahn (American Canal and Transportation Center). This lovingly written guide points out interesting spots along the towpath just about every few feet. It is available at most libraries and some bookstores.

ADC's Washington Area Bike Map. Available at most bookstores.

America's Rail-Trails. Rails-To-Trails Conservancy, 202-797-5400. The Rails-To-Trails Conservancy is spearheading the conversion of abandoned railroads into hiker/biker and recreational trails. Several of the rides in this book are rail trails, and there are over 500 of them across the country.

Arlington County Bikeway Map. Arlington County Department of Public Works, 703-358-3681. Fantastic map to a stupendous system of trails.

Baltimore and Annapolis Trail Park Guide. UMBC Department of Geography, 410-552-6244. Another neat strip map, this colorful guide is available at the B & A Trail Ranger Station at mile 7 on the trail. It has history vignettes keyed to lettered historical markers you see along the trail.

Carroll County Classic Country Bicycle Tours. Carroll County Office of Tourism, 410-857-2983.

A Guide to Montgomery County Parks. Maryland National Capital Park and Planning Commission, 301-495-2525.

A Guide to Parks in Montgomery and Prince George's Counties. Maryland National Capital Park and Planning Commission, 301-495-2525. This brochure tells you everything you need to know about most of the stream valley trails listed in this book. It is available at most MNCPPC parks.

Guide to the Northern Central Railroad Trail. Howling Wolf Publications, 301-589-9455. This is a great strip map and guidebook for the NCRR trail and fun reading even if you never make it to the trail. It is available at bookstores and bike shops, as well as from the publisher.

How to Enjoy Reston, With Facilities and Pathways Map. Reston Association, 703-437-1402.

Howard County Bike and Hike Pathway Map. Howard County Department of Recreation and Parks, 410-313-2770.

Lower Montgomery County Bicycle Route Map. Maryland County Department of Transportation, 301-217-2145.

Northeast Branch Indian Creek Park Trail. Maryland National Capital Park and Planning Commission, 301-699-2407.

Take a Hike—Trails in Montgomery County Parks. Maryland National Capital Park and Planning Commission, 301-495-2525.

Trail Guide—Washington and Old Dominion Regional Park. Northern Virginia Regional Park Authority, 703-729-0596. Yet another strip map, very nicely done.

Bicycle Rental

Bicycle Outfitters, 703-777-6126, in Leesburg.

Big Wheel Bicycles, 703-739-2300, in Old Town Alexandria.

Bike Exchange, 703-768-3444, in Alexandria.

Fletcher's Boathouse, 202-244-0461, on C&O Towpath north of Georgetown.

Monkton Bike Rental, 410-771-4058. Bicycles, trailers and tandems available for rent. Located on the NCRR Trail at Monkton (mile 7.5).

Pedal Pushers, 410-544-2323. Located on the Baltimore and Annapolis Trail in Severna Park at mile 5. Trailers, tandems and even pedal-powered cars available for rent.

Swain's Lock, 301-299-9006, on C&O Towpath north of Great Falls Park, Md.

Thompson's Boat Center, 202-333-9543, located on the Rock Creek Trail, just south of Georgetown.

Bicycling Clubs

Baltimore Bicycling Club, 410-792-8308. The BBC also sponsors the Burley Club, which organizes rides for families with children. Contact Ken Greco at 301-381-0768.

League of American Wheelmen, 410-539-3399. The LAW is the oldest bicycling organization in the U.S., originally formed in the 1800s to lobby for better roads—for cyclists. Despite its sexist name, LAW has as many female as male members. It sponsors two nationwide, week-long cycling festivals each year. It also has a series of regional ride directors who can provide information on cycling rides across the country.

Oxon Hill Bicycle Club, 301-839-4270. A very active club with many older riders.

Potomac Area Council, American Youth Hostels, 202-783-4943. The AYH is the organization that maintains a series of inexpensive places to stay, called hostels, across the country. It also sponsors bicycle rides and other events.

Potomac Pedalers Touring Club, 202-363-TOUR. This is one of the largest cycling clubs in the country, with a wide range of rides. The PPTC cosponsors a summer weekend at Chincoteague with the Baltimore Bicycling Club.

Reston Bicycle Club, 703-758-1000.

Washington Area Bicyclist Association, 202-872-9830. Many of the paths listed in this book are there because WABA lobbied to have them built. WABA is a cycling advocate's organization rather than a touring club, but through it you can keep up with the latest in trail news and help use your political clout to work for new ones.

TO HELP PLAN YOUR TRAVEL IN THE MID-ATLANTIC AREA

THE WALKER WASHINGTON GUIDE   **$8.95**
The seventh edition of the "Guide's guide to Washington,"
completely revised by Katherine Walker, builds on a 25-year
reputation as the top general guide to the capital. Its 320
pages are packed with museums, galleries, hotels, restaurants, theaters, shops, churches, as well as sites. Beautiful
maps and photos. Indispensable.

INNS OF THE BLUE RIDGE   **$11.95**
More than 125 country escapes in six mountain states,
Virginia to Georgia, all personally visited. Selections include country manors, farmhouses, hunting lodges,
B&Bs—a complete range from the luxurious to the laid-
back. Nuts and bolts info tells the what, where, how much
and other details to help make the right choice. Maps and
photos.

MARYLAND ONE-DAY TRIP BOOK   **$10.95**
From boiling rapids and rugged trails high in the western
mountains to frontier forts, horse country, Baltimore's urban
treasures, the Chesapeake Bay and the plantations and pre-
serves of the Eastern Shore, Maryland is more than you can
imagine!

THE WEST VIRGINIA ONE-DAY TRIP BOOK   **$11.95**
Over 150 diverse, affordable day adventures in the magic
mountain state, including excursions to historic mansions,
craft centers, caverns, art museums, Civil War battlefields,
state parks, even a palace of gold and a miniature Swiss
village. Very accessible info on fishing, skiing, white water
rafting. Maps/photos/charts.

ONE-DAY TRIPS THROUGH HISTORY   **$9.95**
Describes 200 historic sites within 150 miles of the nation's
capital where our forebears lived, dramatic events occurred
and America's roots took hold. Sites and arranged chronologi-
cally starting with pre-history.

THE VIRGINIA ONE-DAY TRIP BOOK   **$8.95**
Jane Ockershausen Smith, one of the most experienced travel
writers in the Mid-Atlantic area, admits to being surprised by
the wealth of things to see and do in the Old Dominion. With
101 sites divided into seven geographic regions, this is the
perfect guide for anyone who is anywhere in Virginia.

NORTH CAROLINA ONE-DAY TRIP BOOK   **$11.95**
150 excursions throughout the Tarheel State that beckon day-
trippers of all ages and interest. The state slogan says "The
beauty only begins with the scenery"—we've organized all of
it into seven geographic regions for easy planning, supple-
mented with maps and seasonal information.

Also:

Florida One-Day Trips (from Orlando). What to do after you've done Disney. **$7.95**

Call it Delmarvalous. How to talk, cook and "feel to hum" on the Delaware,
Maryland, and Virginia Peninsula. **$7.95**

A Shunpiker's Guide to the Northeast. Wide open routes that shun turnpikes and
interstates between Washington and Boston. Maps and directions included. **$9.95**

Footnote Washington. Tracking the engaging, humorous and surprising bypaths of
capital history by one of the city's most popular broadcasters. **$8.95**

Walking Tours of Old Washington and Alexandria. Paul Hogarth's exquisite water-
colors of grand old buildings, lovingly reproduced and arranged in seven guided
walking tours. **$24.95**

Order Blank for all EPM books described here. Mail with check to:

EPM Publications, Inc.
Box 490, McLean, VA 22101

Title	Quantity	Price	Amount	Shipping
_____	_____	_____	_____	_____
_____	_____	_____	_____	_____
_____	_____	_____	_____	_____
_____	_____	_____	_____	_____

Subtotal   _____

Virginia residents add 4 1/2% tax   _____

Orders totaling up to $15 add $3.00 shipping/handling   _____

Orders totaling more than $15 add $4.00 first item, $.50 add'l   _____

Name _____

Street _____

City _____ State _____ Zip ____

                                              Total _____

Remember to enclose names, addresses and enclosure cards for gift purchases.
Please note that prices are subject to change. Thank you.

About the Author

John Pescatore began bicycling as soon as his legs grew long enough for his feet to reach the pedals. He has been cycling in the Washington-Baltimore area for 15 years, logging about 1500 miles a year. He can often be seen pulling his daughter Lauren in a trailer on a local trail with his wife Carole and their son Kevin pedaling alongside. Lauren was ten months old for her first bicycle ride, the 22-mile Youghiogheny River Trail tour described in this book.

Pescatore was born in Brooklyn, NY and earned his degree in electric engineering from the University of Connecticut in 1978. He has worked for the Department of Defense and the U.S. Secret Service and is currently the technology manager for GTE in Rockville, MD. He is also a free-lance writer, published in *Bicycling USA*, *Mystery Scene*, *American Hiker*, and *The Washington Times*. His articles on family bicycling have appeared in regional parenting magazines across the country. He lives in Ashton, MD with Carole, Kevin, Lauren and a garage full of bicycles.